The Cultural Myth of
Masculinity

THE CULTURAL MYTH OF
MASCULINITY

Chris Blazina

Westport, Connecticut
London

Library of Congress Cataloging-in-Publication Data

Blazina, Christopher.
    The cultural myth of masculinity / Chris Blazina.
      p. cm.
    Includes bibliographical references and index.
    ISBN 0–275–97990–3
      1. Masculinity—History.   2. Men—Socialization—History.   I. Title.
HQ1090.B545 2003
305.31′09—dc21   2002193130

British Library Cataloguing in Publication Data is available.

Library of Congress Catalog Card Number: 2002193130
ISBN: 0–275–97990–3

First published in 2003

Praeger Publishers, 88 Post Road West, Westport, CT 06881
An imprint of Greenwood Publishing Group, Inc.
www.praeger.com

Printed in the United States of America

The paper used in this book complies with the
Permanent Paper Standard issued by the National
Information Standards Organization (Z39.48–1984).

10 9 8 7 6 5 4 3 2 1

For the men who have enriched my life—
And for Kelsey

CONTENTS

ACKNOWLEDGMENTS

I would like to thank those individuals who supported me throughout this project. This includes a special thanks to Dov Liberman for his assistance in making this a more readable manuscript. Thanks to Jim Mahalik, Ed Willems, and Stewart Pisecco for reviewing the manuscript and for the invaluable feedback that oftentimes pulled me out of the theoretical fog. Thanks to Dora Soublis, who assisted me in preparing the manuscript. Thanks to Ed Watkins for his encouragement to finish this book. Finally, thanks to my father and his C-Span dream.

INTRODUCTION

While the study of gender roles has only been officially recognized as a science since the rise of nineteenth-century sexology and psychoanalysis, it is reasonable to conclude that guidelines for men's gender-appropriate behavior have been of concern for some time. To that end, this book is devoted to the historical analysis of how, in Western culture, the concept of masculinity has been defined and then redefined over the centuries. To some readers, the notion that masculinity has been anything but a constant throughout history may be surprising. However, both Pleck (1981) and Connell (1995) have suggested that masculinity has had different meanings and definitions over time. That is, there has been fluidity to its definition. For example, in *History of Sexuality* (1980), historian Michel Foucault discusses the concept of masculine gender roles in ancient Greece, where beauty was the guiding ethos for finding a romantic partner desirable, irrespective of the person's gender. Further, what was considered to be normative behavior for boys until they reached puberty would be considered effeminate by contemporary stereotypical standards.

In addition, some scholars have speculated that Cretan prepubescent boys of affluent families participated in a ritual wherein they were abducted by a mentor who paid a "dowry" to the parents for the boy (Sergent, 1984). The two would journey to the woods for a period of two months, during which hunting and feasting occurred. The older male would teach the boy certain skills deemed necessary to be a man. There has been some speculation that this initiation took on a sexual aspect, in which the boy was either literally or figuratively sodomized in order to inject the older man's masculine spirit into the neophyte. After this, the older male would present the boy with three gifts: a military outfit, an ox, and a goblet. Each carried significant meaning. The military outfit indicated that the boy was ready for service as a man. The newly initiated would sacrifice the ox to Zeus and hold a feast. Finally, the goblet symbolized the boy's entrance into manhood by demonstrating his ability to participate in the banquet. Women, children, and barbarians did not drink wine, only men did. Not to participate in this ritual, given that one was handsome and had a good ancestral lineage, was considered disgraceful and a sign of bad character. Even after the ritual was complete, the former mentor would send gifts and clothing to his initiate, and those who were initiated were held in special honor. By juxtaposing this more ancient definition of masculinity and its processes of socialization to current cultural values for men, we can see that, historically, masculinity has not been not a constant concept.

The focus of this book is to examine the cultural myth of masculinity; that is, the socially constructed notions of the masculine ideal that occurred in a specific culture within a specific timeframe. A culture's standards and ideals in regard to gender roles can be studied through examining very tangible forms of cultural expression. We do this by exploring two forms of myths: (1) the stories of gods and heroes, and (2) paradigms of male socialization. It is recognized from the onset that this study of masculinity and its tools is within Western culture and that the consequent conclusions may not be applicable outside of this realm.

The first type of myth used in our analysis—the stories of gods and heroes—will demonstrate how these mythical figures act as prototypes for men's behavior. These figures are icons that stem from notions of what the culture considers prototypical masculine ideals. These span the gamut from a loving god or hero whose weapon is peace and whose behavior consists of turning the other cheek to a bellicose warrior who seeks everlasting fame for deeds of courage. In any case, these are images that men can point to as models to emulate.

It is important to bring a contextual interpretation to these mythic expressions and icons. For instance, there is currently a plethora of books, seminars, and workshops that use so-called ancient mythology as a means to describe and prescribe how both men and women should be in contemporary times. In most cases, these contemporary interpretations of ancient themes do not take into account the contexts in which the myths were created and thus often misinterpret their original meanings. They also tend to be highly selective in stressing aspects of the myths that fit their paradigms and to neglect the big-picture perspective of the sociocultural forces that created the original myths in the first place. For example, to speak of ancient Greek myths as models for men today is to lose the significance of when and how they were originally created and for what purpose.

The cultural myth of masculinity is also expressed in the paradigms of thought that are adopted. Most specifically, we will focus on the paradigms that showcase culturally specific templates for male socialization and, from them, the rules for how men should conduct themselves on a day-to-day basis. These paradigms of socialization offer the social cement of a culture in the context of gender roles. They constitute the rulebook for what is gender-appropriate behavior, including currently sanctioned definitions and standards, how to go about achieving those standards, what type of behavior violates the norm, and how to raise young boys to become culturally appropriate men. These models for male socialization can be found in paradigms of thought such as chivalry, sexology, and psycho-analysis. They are also specific to a given time period and must be inter-preted in a contextual manner so as not to lose their original meaning. These paradigms of socialization are referred to as myths because they are, at least to some extent, socially constructed. At times, each has been embraced as objective reality only to be later questioned and either altered or completely replaced.

We are seeking an understanding of masculine ideals reflecting Western myth, rather than a description of the reality of what men have achieved in a particular society. This distinction is important, for while cultural myths showcase our prototypes of how it should be, they may not always easily approximate achievable reality. For instance, one may strive to act as the Nordic/Germanic myths tell us, to be cool-headed even unto painful death, to go so far as to make clever quips upon dying. However, can we take these examples of myths to say that all men in that culture died in this fashion, with such unflappability? Probably not. Rather, the myth represents an ideal. Some may approximate it; even fewer achieve it; but, certainly, many feel compelled to attempt to live up to it. That is, there is a prescriptive aspect of myth in that it gives societal members an ideal model for how one should strive to be.

Along this line, Connell (1995) has argued for the consideration of the concept of hegemony, which refers to "the cultural dynamic by which a group claims and sustains a leading position in social life" (p. 77). Connell applies the concept of hegemony to the notion of masculinity. He argues there will always be one exalted definition, or form, of masculinity within a culture and that members of that culture will be influenced by it, if not compelled to emulate it. As is true with other cultural dynamics, a small but influential group is responsible for setting many of the hegemonic norms regarding masculinity. This group may consist of political leaders, rulers, the wealthy sector of the society, and the like. For example, the small group consisting of the warrior/aristocracy culture of the Middle Ages established a hegemonic notion of chivalric masculinity that became a dominant cultural ideal. The dominant paradigm of masculinity can also be influenced by real individuals or by fantasy figures such as mythic heroes. Thus the example of chivalric masculinity during the Middle Ages applies as well to the John Wayne masculinity of the twentieth century. In the latter case, masculine icons are based upon characters in movies, not necessarily upon the actual men who played them.

In building upon Connell's (1995) notion of hegemonic masculinity, we see that a culture has one dominant set of masculine ideals that are reflected within the most dominant forms of mythology. (This includes stories of gods and heroes as well as male socialization paradigms.) Therefore, we expect in our examination of myth to see these masculine ideals highlighted or reinforced. A note of caution must accompany this approach. At any time within a given culture, there may exist other less-prominent sets of masculine paradigms that may not be found within the dominant model of masculine mythology. For instance, in chapter 6, "Psychology's Myth of Masculinity," we examine how Clatterbaugh (1998) highlights numerous competing models of masculinity that exist within contemporary Western culture. Some scholars may argue that, as opposed to the dominant paradigm, these models receive very little play in current discussions of male mythology.

In considering how the construction and reconstruction of the hegemonic cultural myth of masculinity occurs, we look to the Hegelian dialectic model as a guide. Most notably, historian of science Thomas Kuhn (1962) has used the dialectic model in explaining how dominant scientific paradigms wax and wane in terms of levels of influence (later, we shall see that other scholars have employed this same model to explain the changes in "masculinity" over time).

The dialectic thesis-antithesis-synthesis approach stresses the notion that at any given time a dominant paradigm of thought or science exists. This model will stay in place as long as it can sustain its position, oftentimes beyond its real level of usefulness, until there is more than enough reason to believe it has been disproved. The dialectic process argues that rival competing models will attempt to oust it. Tension is created when the dominant model is in jeopardy and the competing models jockey for the place of prominence. If the older paradigm is successful in this process, it will be able to account for or adapt to challenges to its underlying premises. However, if the challenger is successful, a synthesis process will occur whereby a new dominant model is adopted. This new way of thinking is uniquely different from the paradigms before it.

This dialectic process can be applied to our understanding of the fluid nature of masculine paradigms as well (Connell, 1995; Pleck, 1981). The dominant masculine paradigms are constructed in a similar dialectic manner. Models are created, challenged, and replaced over time. This is an ongoing process that leads to the fluid condition of what is considered masculine within a culture. While inspired by Kuhn's use of the Hegelian dialectic, my approach differs from his in one significant way. Kuhn's emphasis is upon paradigms competing and, eventually, one model's entirely replacing another. My emphasis is upon how cultural paradigms of masculinity compete and are replaced while still allowing for the blending of material from the old model with the new one. That is, the old paradigm of masculinity does not entirely disappear. If compatible, aspects of the old paradigm continue in the new hegemonic model. This new model continues its cultural task by providing masculine icons and methods of socialization for men.

The dominant paradigm of masculinity is reflected in cultural mythology, in both the resulting hero icons and the rules for male socialization. By looking at these tangible reflections, we can examine what a culture holds as its prototypical masculine ideals. Furthermore, when the dominant model of masculinity is challenged by another paradigm, both the tension and the movement toward resolution can be tracked through the same expressions of cultural mythology. In this way, we can contextually follow what the dominant models of masculinity are and when they are in the process of change.

Inspired by the dialectic process, the dominant cultural myth of masculinity changes in two ways: (1) the old paradigm outlives its usefulness, and (2) competing paradigms interface. As mentioned earlier, oftentimes when a guiding myth or paradigm is displaced, it is because the evidence against it is more than sufficient to do so. The influence of the old paradigm and its supporters and, perhaps, a fear of the chaos and the acceptance of the untested may keep the old paradigm in place for longer than merited. For instance, a contemporary analysis reveals a questioning of current masculine templates and how some of them have fallen out of favor. There are current, ongoing questions about the applicability of the twentieth-century gender-role models, which include the John Wayne–type masculinity popular since World War II.

In order to understand how masculine myths change by outliving their usefulness, it is important to appreciate changing sociocultural forces.

New sociocultural forces may call for men to respond to the pressing needs of the culture in new ways. When this occurs, there can be changes in what is considered the ideal masculinity. A case in point would be wartime versus peacetime notions of prototypical masculinity. The needs of the culture push for differing notions of appropriate masculinity. What is suggested here is that the culture plays a significant role in the shaping of what is considered appropriate gender roles. Gender roles do not change solely as a result of the intrapsychic needs of the men of the community. That is, men do not feel that their ideal is no longer suitable and so the ideal simply changes. Rather, there is an interface of the people who make the myths with the culture's current climate.

Beyond this, shifts in the cultural myth of masculinity also occur due to the interaction of competing cultural paradigms and ideas, with the end product being a "new" synthesis of masculinity. Thus, the process of change can ensue when models simultaneously compete within the culture for the dominant position. The change process may also occur when a model of masculinity is introduced from outside the culture and competes with one from within the culture. However, in both cases, when there is a new synthesis of masculinity, not all aspects of the old paradigms are necessarily erased. The very process of synthesis causes some aspects of the old paradigm of masculinity to be a part of the newer synthesis. This is not to say that each cultural paradigm is an equal partner in the development of a new model. Rather, there is a dominant paradigm that incorporates aspects of another less-influential but still prominent paradigm. This leads to a shuffle of cultural mythology, which includes a shift in the cultural icons and in methods of male socialization.

Looking at how paradigms compete simultaneously within a culture, we can again examine contemporary models of masculinity whereby the prominent notion of an ideal man's being a warrior was challenged after the Vietnam War. The "sensitive man" model of the 1970s attempted to oust it. A prominent example of cultural paradigms interfacing is the creation of classical Greek mythology. Classical scholars argue that nomadic Indo-Europeans of 2500 B.C.E. interacted with and subdued the pre-Hellenic peoples of what would become modern-day Greece, creating a pantheon of gods that constituted a compromise between the two cultures. This resulted in the blending of a culture dominated by a male sky god with one dominated by an earth goddess. While the pre-Hellenic earth goddess in the new mix occupied a lower status than she formerly enjoyed, her presence altered the gender-role paradigms for both men and women.

Masculinity as a paradigm has seen prior evolutions and in all likelihood will continue to do so. In taking this stance, we will explore the forces that shape the cultural myth of masculinity. Connell (1995) has suggested that "to understand gender we must constantly go beyond gender" (p. 76). To that end, notions of masculine prototypes, economy, class structure, previous history, and the dialectic forces of culture are not only fair game but are essential to the understanding of the evolving paradigm of masculinity. They all reflect the cultural myth of masculinity. In chapters 1–6 of this book, we will directly examine masculine ideals and important evolutions of these ideals across time. In chapter 7, we will draw conclusions about this line of inquiry.

Vital to our understanding of the cultural myth of masculinity is the appreciation of what many scholars have recognized as the tripartite division of Western culture. There are three separate but interrelated social divisions, and each has its own definition of ideal masculinity. First, we traditionally see the king/aristocracy/religious orders at the highest social rung, and they have their own version of ideal masculinity based mostly on nobility and refinement. These notions speak to a "more evolved" person whose nobility allows him to rule or govern others. Second, we see the warrior caste, whose idea of masculinity includes notions of honor, action, and bellicosity. Much of our discussion centers on a dialectic competition between these two models throughout Western culture. This tension is reflected in the contextual myths we will review. Finally, the third caste comprises the sustenance providers upon whose labors the other two castes reside. We will see that masculine ideals from this caste seem to play a prominent role in attempting to define more contemporary notions of Western masculinity.

As we examine the structure of Western culture, so also we must study some of its important evolutions. This, of course, has direct bearing upon changing notions and paradigms of ideal masculinity. We will begin our examination with a brief overview of Proto-Indo-European (PIE) culture, which is believed by many scholars to be the prototypical beginnings of Western culture. The warrior ethic found in the PIE culture plays a large part in the foundation of Western masculinity. Its importance and its defining characteristics, such as honor and character, which can be summed up as *kléos aphthitos,* "the fame that does not decay" (see Lincoln, 1991), are discussed. We add to this understanding when we consider the definition of masculinity that comes from the ruling aristocracy. The notion of refinement (on many levels) is believed to reflect, according to this mythos, a more ordered and higher evolution of man. These two masculinities are the masculine paradigms that Western cultures have most extensively embraced.

From there, we will move into the Middle Ages, where the old Indo-European warrior ethic is infused with Judeo-Christian religion. The paradigm shifts, and the hardened warrior is challenged to become, instead, a softened chivalrous and courtly gentleman. This reflects an ongoing cultural tension between the two masculinities represented on the one hand by the warrior, on the other by the nobleman. We will see that this tension is reflected in the creation of the chivalric mythos of the day. This new mythology is an attempt to blend aspects from each of the two social classes that Western culture seems to value the most. We will see that this cultural task does not have a definite resolution other than to dichotomize already-existing battle lines.

Finally, the evolution of Western masculinity moves further, as the aristocratic and warrior ethic becomes the basis for the definition of masculinity within the burgeoning middle class. We will see that the cultural riddle of attempting to blend the two masculinities is a task that the middle-class model attempts to solve. Our examination will include contemporary middle-class notions and the factors that contributed to the model's construction. Because the middle class is a relatively new social status (emerging from the sixteenth to the eighteenth centuries), we must undertake the task of exploring the elements of the preexisting social classes from which it borrowed in constructing its template of masculinity. This is done through examining the masculine ideals of the ruling aristocracy and of arms-bearing warriors. We can then follow the thread through the cultural reconstructions and evolutions of the cultural myth that will eventually lead to the current hegemonic notion of masculinity. These paradigms and ideals become the blueprints for modern Western masculinity and are reflected and cocreated in the studies of sexology, psychoanalysis, and gender-role paradigms. This, the stuff of which the contemporary models of masculinity are made, will help us see how the current masculine ideal is represented in mythic form. From this perspective, we turn now to examine the cultural myth of masculinity and its roots.

Chapter 1

THE INDO-EUROPEANS

In this chapter, we explore the prototypal roots of Western masculinity, the warrior and then the ruling aristocracy in Proto-Indo-European (PIE) culture. While there have been subsequent evolutions and changes in this concept in the daughter languages and cultures, it is from this original stuff that Western culture is formed. Therefore, an examination of the PIE cultural myth represents an examination of the basic building blocks that will lead to the formation of Western masculinity.

The term *Indo-European* refers to a language group from which the Germanic, Nordic, Indic, Italic, Slavic, Baltic, Armenian, Albanian, and Celtic languages arose. Currently, the speakers of Indo-European languages make up nearly half the world's population. Because language is such an important carrier of a culture's ideology and values, some scholars have argued that elements of the prototypical Western culture still remain in these present-day daughter languages and cultures. Among these, the eminent Indo-European studies scholar Georges Dumézil (1970, 1973) has argued that the core of this PIE culture has survived even in the midst of cultural mixing across the millennia. Anthropologist Scott Littleton (1982) has argued that the part of this core that helped shape medieval Europe's feudal system survived into the thoughts of the framers of the U.S. Constitution and has taken on even more prominence over the last few centuries. Littleton (1982) has gone as far as to suggest that studying the Indo-Europeans "is to study the ultimate source of most of our own (Western) community's values and worldview. For after all due credit is given to the Near Eastern and other sources of our tradition, we Westerners are still for the most part I-E speakers" (Littleton, 1982, p. 236).

Aspects of the PIE culture are still very much an integral part of our modern Western consciousness. Though some 6,000 years separate the PIE peoples from us today, their cultural themes, though sometimes altered, reworked, and recycled, still carry lasting impact. Their influence includes implicit and explicit messages about how men define what is masculine within Western culture.

THE PROTO-INDO-EUROPEANS

There have been many debates over the origins and existence of a PIE culture from which Indo-European languages and cultural themes arose. It was not until 1786 that Sir William Jones postulated a PIE language and with it a PIE people who spoke it (Lincoln, 1991). He maintained that linguistic paleontology, archaeology, and mythological evidence support the existence of a PIE people. Gimbutas (1989, 1991) has suggested that waves of these Indo-European peoples began to move across the European continent from what is believed to be their homeland in the Caspian steppes in what is today southern Russia. In three waves, the first from 4300 to 4200 B.C.E., the second from 3400 to 3200 B.C.E., and the third from 3000 to 2800 B.C.E., they eventually reached as far south as the Mediterranean Sea, as far east as India, as far north as Iceland, and as far west as Ireland. During their heyday, they ruled over the territory stretching from India to Iceland (Lincoln, 1991). Their journeys impacted the very foundations of Western civilizations (Baring & Cashford, 1993; Littleton, 1982; Puhvel, 1987; Ruck & Staples, 1994).

While Lincoln (1991) has suggested that each of the Indo-European daughter languages and cultures would subsequently be influenced by its varying surroundings (e.g., the indigenous peoples the cultures encountered, economics, climate, and so forth), thus forming its own unique persona or cultural myth, each still carried a part of the original, core culture. What is argued here is that a part of that core that has remained relates to aspects of gender identity that shape the present-day gender roles of men.

BATTLE AXE CULTURE

As the Indo-European peoples came under historical scrutiny, they were seen as aggressive warriors riding two abreast in horse-drawn chariots. They are described by some scholars as the "corded ware" culture (referring

to the pottery of the period) and also as the "battle axe" culture (referring
to their weapons and penchant for bellicosity).

> The battle axe cultures represent the roots of the Indo-European speaking
> peoples. . . . What can be said with some certainty is that the battle axe
> people had a large ethnic, social, and cultural inheritance from the hunter-
> fishers of the forest cultures. . . . Though it may not always or everywhere
> have been so, this character came in to be dominantly pastoral, patriarchal,
> warlike and expansive. (Hawkes, 1958, p. 31)

Winn (1995) has cautioned that the corded ware society was not necessarily identical with the PIE culture but certainly reflected many of the
cultural ideals its members held. Crucial among these was the importance
of honor and character. Haudry (1999) has supported these descriptors of
the PIE culture:

> We behold a proud and warlike aristocracy, partial to life, wide open spaces,
> the goods of the world and above all fame, whose peace-time leisure is
> devoted to animal raising, equestrian sports, and hunting; an aristocracy for
> which "character" (ménos) is a man's essential quality, and "fame" (kléwos)
> the chief goal of his existence. (p. 16)

Eisler (1988) has suggested the PIE culture is the prototypical "blade"
society, which engaged in continuous conflict not only with the peoples
that surrounded them but also with one another. It has been suggested that
the warriors accompanied by members of the priestly caste would invade
an area, conquer it, and then rule the indigenous population of each land.
Given the priests' accompaniment of the warriors, there is some speculation that these invasions may have been religious crusades as well as
territorial conquests. Lincoln (1991) has suggested that religion may have
not been the ultimate cause of war and raiding but that the two were
intimately intertwined.

Adding to the notion of the importance of the warrior ethic, Haudry
(1999) has suggested that there was only one acceptable way of life—to
be a warrior. The society was also demarcated by age gradations in relation
to the warrior ethic. There were four different distinctions of men based
upon their physical ability to bear arms: boys (too young to bear arms),
young warriors, elder warriors (both of which bore arms), and older men
(too old to bear arms).

Although an important part of the society, the warrior is a constant
worry because he has the potential to overstep the bounds of his bellicosity
(Dumézil, 1970). Even good warriors were liable to fall into wrongdoing.

To accomplish the fame that does not decay through his warring actions, the warrior had to dehumanize his opponent as well as himself in battle, thus eradicating human qualities of compassion, remorse, and guilt (Lincoln, 1991). This issue is more fully discussed in chapter 2, on heroes and zanes, as Indo-European heroes such as Achilles and Hercules commit the "sins of the warrior" who go too far in their battle rage. For these fallen heroes, there is sometimes an opportunity for redemption through action that purifies the wrong deeds.

INDO-EUROPEAN ATTITUDE

Linton (1957) and Lincoln (1991) have observed that while there was some limited agriculture, the Indo-European economy was mostly based on herding and cattle. Linton suggests that this type of economy led to the development of aristocratic-type social patterns in which leaders or chieftains arose in the tribe according to their wealth and power, which were directly related to their holdings and number of supporters. While this sets the tone for subsequent methods of gaining prestige, it also speaks to the potential for social mobility. Pearson (1973) has suggested that while there was some limited social mobility in PIE culture, there was a premium upon endogamy, wherein members of the same aristocracy intermarried. This allowed for a more secure base of power and influence, to be maintained by the social elite. What social mobility was present was hard fought for and was guided by the achievement of heroic deeds. For instance, in the ancient Germanic culture, a newly made noble's family was not fully absorbed into that class until his grandson's generation. As Haudry (1999) has noted, this is difficult to know for certain. However, it is reasonable to embrace the notion that the fame that does not decay was obtained through both ancestral lineage and the deeds of the present warrior. Warriors could improve the prestige of their family name through acts of courage. Improving social and economic standing might occur after the battle, when the chief would award the bravest warriors with the best spoils, that is, the hero's portion. The most valued award was an item coming from the chief himself. Another method of gaining fame was the result of the nature of the economy, which held a special place of honor for the successful cattle raider (Lincoln, 1991). It is believed that the Indo-Europeans used horse-drawn chariots in battle as well as in their raids. This gave them a distinct advantage over the non-Indo-European peoples they raided.

Fate also played a powerful role in the destiny of the warrior's mobility in that it had dominion over gods as well as men. For PIE cultural descendants, *destiny* in this sense carries the meaning of "portion" or "gift" (Haudry, 1999). Palmer (1956) has suggested that "each component of the universe, gods, man and natural objects, has its allotted portion, the boundaries of which might not be transgressed without grave result" (p. 258). Therefore, we see in Indo-European cultures such as the Germanic, the Greek, and the Vedic Indian a respect for caste. This does not mean however, that respecting one's lot bars one from moving up the social ladder. This concept of allotted portion resigned the Indo-European warrior to the ills of fate but also effused within him the knowledge he could overcome even the hatred of the gods if it were his fate to do so. Thus a strong sense of individualism arose, typified by a striving for glory.

A part of the successful warrior is a psychology of action (Haudry, 1999). One was to strive for mastery over the self through avoiding behavioral excess; undisciplined wandering of the mind; excess words; and brutal, inconsiderate acts. These characteristics are reflected in the actions of the warrior in that he was to think, speak, and act well. Equally important as actually possessing these qualities was having someone speak well of them on a warrior's behalf. It is believed (Haudry, 1999) that there is a strong shame-based quality to the Indo-European culture, both historically and today. That is, one's identity was created and maintained in the context of the community. To act out of step with communal values was to shame oneself, one's family name, and one's lineage. In the same way, to perform heroic deeds was to bring glory to them. This led to the development of the powerful—and sometimes dreaded—balladeer. At feasts, one might have a paid bard sing the warrior's praises in a form of eulogy listing his accomplishments. This entertained the listeners as well as spread the warrior's fame. The kings also took full advantage of this by having paid bards sing their praises and cajole their rivals.

The heroic characters mentioned could be further clarified by examining the Nordic/Germanic tribes who are the linguistic and cultural descendants of the PIE peoples. Their PIE roots are reflected in the fact that they were patriarchal in social structure, led by fierce warriors who honored the blade and worshiped a sky, mountain, or thunder god. H. R. Ellis Davidson (1965) has characterized the myths that reflect the values of the Nordic/ Germanic people:

> The myths are very much stories of individuals and their reactions to one another; they show lonely gods going their willful ways, with certain responsibilities to the community or the family to which they belong, but little more to hold them. . . . We realize anew the value they set on individualism. . . . The emphasis in the myths is the same as that in the

heroic poetry, on the importance of not holding onto life at any cost, but acting in a way which will be long remembered when life is over. . . . The man who could make a joke when wounded to death or gasp out a witty remark when men were removing an arrow from his throat after battle is honored in the sagas, because even in pain and weakness he could still keep his sense of proportion, and it is this sense which is perhaps the great quality of these northern stories. (pp. 215–217)

Further, the Nordic/Germanic peoples knew they lived on the razor's edge and that a sudden snowstorm, the precarious sea, or a chance encounter with another warrior could end their lives quickly. They valued their individualism and would rather surrender their lives than their values. There arises a noble picture of these peoples who, faced with the specter of death on a constant basis, resigned to live life within the realization of the distinct possibility of death. Davidson (1965) notes that there is no bitterness at the harshness of life, "but rather a spirit of heroic resignation" (p. 218) that carries them through tight places while seeking a glory that will outlive death. Many of these favored characteristics helped define modern Western masculinity even in the nineteenth and twentieth centuries. Masculinity was defined not just by how a man lived but also by how he died, his courage and achievements living on after his glorious death and his deeds being retold by balladeers for generations to come. The retelling of these stories acts as a social template guiding the warrior as well as the masculine neophytes in how to act in proper ways. As we will see, the hardened ways of the warrior were recycled later in the form of the chivalrous knight, in stories of the cowboy in nineteenth- and twentieth-century literature, and in the gender identity model that guided nineteenth- and twentieth-century models for masculinity.

These Indo-European/Germanic/Nordic warriors were not without their downfalls. These included a "tendency toward lack of compassion for the weak, an over-emphasis on material success, and arrogant self-confidence" (Davidson, 1965, p. 219). We will see that similar criticisms would help contribute to the rethinking of the traditional paradigm of masculinity held in the later part of the twentieth century.

TRIPARTITE SOCIETY

The PIE continuing impact can be seen in the mythologies of PIE linguistic and cultural descendants including, among others, Celtic, Germanic, Nordic, Slavic, Indic, and Baltic peoples. Dumézil has proposed that each of these Indo-European cultures could be organized around a tripartite social structure (Dumézil, 1970, 1973). Dumézil (1973) has concluded that at the top of the ranking is the king/priestly caste, whose members are concerned with the maintenance of magico-religious and judicial functions such as the use of magic, religious practices, conducting sacrifices, divining, performing marriages, and so forth. The second caste in order of importance is the warrior caste, which is concerned with physical prowess, fighting monsters, and leading armies. The third and least important caste is that of those who are in charge of providing physical sustenance by maintaining plant and animal fertility. Oftentimes, the indigenous peoples of Europe constitute the third caste.

Dumézil has argued for the existence of a "war of the functions" in that the mythology reflects not only the tripartite aspect of the culture mentioned above but also the existing tension between the first two castes and the third (Dumézil, 1970, 1973). These themes have been discussed further by Lincoln (1991), Littleton (1982), and Mallory (1991). Some scholars argue that this cultural tension is actually a reflection of the territories that the PIE culture (as represented by the first two castes) ultimately subdued and incorporated.

A series of myths highlighted this process between the opposing cultures and castes. The myths show how the conflict was resolved symbolically by blending together cultural myths, with the victor at the summit of society and the subdued in a lesser place. For instance, in the Nordic/Germanic myths, we see the gods of the earth (the Vanir) in conflict with those of the sky (the Aesir). We also see in Roman myth the raping of the Sabine women, who are taken by the ancestors of the Romans and forcefully incorporated into their culture.

Other prominent examples of the cultural interface include the movement of Indo-Europeans into the Mediterranean. In about 2500 B.C.E., waves of Indo-Europeans moving across the European continent reached what is today Greece and the surrounding areas (Baring & Cashford, 1993; Ruck & Staples, 1994). These seminomadic warrior tribes brought with them a patrifocal mythology that included the worship of a sky god— Zeus. They encountered the matrifocal, pre-Greek peoples who were settled in cities and had an economy that was more agrarian in nature. These pre-Greek peoples worshiped an earth-mother goddess. It has been suggested that classical Greek mythology reflects the tensions between the two clashing cultures (Baring & Cashford; Highwater, 1991; Ruck & Staples; Spretnak, 1978). As the Indo-Europeans began to dominate the area, the patrifocal mythology began to usurp the mother-goddess stories, relegating the once-powerful mother goddess to a subservient role.

Scholars such as Highwater (1991) have suggested that the mother goddess myths/religions were occupants of the dark, enclosed spaces of the earth—their prominent symbols being the snake and birds—with the mother goddess assuming the titles "mistress of the beasts" and "snake goddess." The Indo-Europeans, in contrast, were ruled by the god of light, who resided above the earth in the mountains, the volcanoes, and the sky. From the conquering Indo-Europeans' perspective, the foreign ways of these indigenous peoples came to be considered threatening, backward, and barbaric.

One may see the cultural tensions that arose from these differing approaches interwoven into the plays and myths of ancient Greece; for example, in the story of Medea, who helped her husband Jason to fame (including the capturing of the Golden Fleece) through the use of her magic. This is done at no small cost to Medea. (The cost includes her turning against her own father.) Later, Jason wishes to become king of Corinth, and in a political maneuver decides to shun Medea and instead marry Glauke, the daughter of the ruler Kreon. This deeply offends Medea. To spite Jason, Medea eventually kills their children. The same magic that helped Jason gain fame is now aimed at him and his bride-to-be. For instance, Medea sends a magic robe and crown to the bride using her own (Medea's) children as the messengers. When Glauke tries on these items, she, her father, and the wedding guests go mad (in some versions, they burst into flames).

Medea, of course, was not Greek; rather, she was a product of the old world of the pre-Greeks (non-Indo-Europeans). This is demonstrated by the fact that in productions of the play she was clothed as a witch foreigner.

Another example of this new compromise between the old, pre-Greek ways and the Indo-Europeans can be seen in the cult of Dionysus. Women were allowed to return to their pre-Greek customs once a year and make a journey to the wilderness for the religious rites of the old ways. These were considered barbarian acts to the more civilized Greek mind. The Greeks believed these rituals to include women going into frenzies of ecstasy that could include tearing apart live animals and killing and eating children. These stories kept some of the threads of the earlier earth-centered culture but highlighted them in a way that was vastly overexaggerated.

Classical Greek myths can also be interpreted from the perspective of the mother goddess and her children's being challenged, then defeated, by the deputies of the sky god—Zeus. The list of the mother goddess's defeats and transformation are numerous and lengthy. For example, Athena in her earlier form was hermaphroditic and associated with non-matrimonial sexuality. She is transformed in the new order from the cult goddess into the asexual tomboy goddess born not from a woman, but instead from the head of her new father, Zeus. In this way, she is detached from the carnal pleasures of the body and from her former identity. In another example, Hera, the matriarch of the pre-Greeks, is transformed into an overbearing wife who is out for revenge on Zeus and all of his sexual conquests. This eventually evolved into the story of Hercules. Hercules' name, ironically, means "glory of Hera." In the story, Hercules, the deputy of Zeus, defeats the creatures associated with the pre-Greek goddess religion. He is the great-grandson of Perseus, who himself did much damage to the goddess and her deputies, including Medusa, the snake-headed Gorgon. Over the course of his career, Hercules would take up where his great-grandfather left off and conquer the "monsters" of nature associated with the goddess. These included, among others, the seven-headed Hydra, the boar of Mount Erymanthos (symbol for the goddess consort), and the Nemean lion.

Another example of this process of transformation is the myth of Apollo, the youthful god of light. In the Greek mind, Apollo came to represent the manly and civilized characteristics of order and tamed instincts (Highwater, 1991). He was the "new" oracle at Delphi, who used his prophetic clarity to see into the future and make sense of the chaos of life. As a boy god, Apollo wandered the world looking for a place to call home, eventually deciding on Delphi. Of course, it was no small coincidence that he chose Delphi, for in the evolution of mythology, prominent symbols or shrines of the former mythos must somehow be incorporated into the newer, evolving mythic order. In this case, the matrifocal mythos of Gaia at Delphi needed to be incorporated into the patrifocal system represented by Apollo. In the matrifocal mythos, Delphi was not only the home of Gaia but also of her daughter Python, the snake goddess. (Some stories tell that Hera created Python—Hera being yet another form of the mother goddess.) Python was a child of the earth who lived in darkness, symbolizing to the Greeks all the uncivilized passions and chaos associated with the matrifocal culture and, eventually, women. Apollo could not claim Delphi until he defeated its inhabitant (the symbolic form of Gaia), which he did by killing Python with his arrows of light, illuminating the Greek culture by lifting it out of barbarism and solidifying the patrifocal shift of power (Highwater, 1991). However, Apollo's victory was not complete. Whenever Apollo was not present at Delphi, Dionysus, an earthy and at times effeminate god closely aligned with the mother goddess, sat in his place.

What should be noted in all of these stories, myths, and tales is that, though altered in terms of appearance and status, the goddess symbols were not erased. Rather, they remained a prominent fixture (although now used as a foil) of the new cultural myth. On one level, they represent the political tensions of an Indo-European culture clashing with that of a non-Indo-European one. This included an attempted resolution of matrifocal conflicts, which arose when the Indo-Europeans conquered and attempted to assimilate the indigenous peoples into their own culture and ideology.

One must consider the psychology of the PIE culture to place these cultural tensions in proper perspective. The Greek Indo-European mind considered the non-Indo-Europeans as barbaric and a number of their characteristics as feminine and therefore unacceptable to men. These characteristics included chaos and passion (Blazina, 1997). Whether they be the three-headed monster of the early cattle cycle or the snake goddess of the pre-Greeks, those cultural elements considered as foreign take on a monstrous persona. This has implications for the men of antiquity as well as for contemporary Western culture. Those aspects that are considered foreign to the hegemonic prototype also take on a pejorative persona—being unmanly, untrustworthy—and are to be avoided or controlled. An inevitable extension in more contemporary times would be homophobia and the fear of the feminine.

CATTLE SAGA

As mentioned previously, mythology reflected the tension between the differing sects within the tripartite culture. This is sometimes referred to as the "war of the functions." In this war, whether symbolic on the mythological level, or acted out in some type of real battle, the PIE cultures come out as the victor. This is reflected within the first two levels of the tripartite society, which encompasses the king/priestly caste and the warrior class, both consisting of Indo-Europeans. The third function is made up of sustenance providers and is believed to be the non-Indo-European indigenous peoples. The third caste is soundly defeated in the war of functions and takes an integral but subservient role in the society. The king became the embodied culmination of all three functions of the culture and, therefore, the highest evolutionary figure of Indo-European society. To that end, the myth of the cattle saga, upon which the Indo-European theme of warrior-hero rests, will be examined. Then, the importance of the king in the society will be traced in Indo-European creation myth. What should be noted here is the importance of class, even in this ancient setting. There were differing expectations for a member of the warrior class, for those who were more aligned with the political/ideological class, and for those who provided basic sustenance for the culture. We will see the impact of these class distinctions on differing definitions of masculinity.

Several important mitigating factors influenced the development of the cultural myth of masculinity among the Indo-European peoples. A prominent one, certainly, was that the Indo-Europeans were mainly breeders of livestock and cattle, though it is now believed that they had some agricultural interest as well. As Linton (1957) observes, "A cattle people cannot choose but be warlike" (p. 257). They must constantly be on guard for potential thieves, and they themselves add to their own herds by stealing the cattle of others. A successful cattle thief was (or may have been) among the most admired members of the community.

The paramount importance of cattle is seen in one of the earliest Indo-European myths involving the first cattle raid (Mallory, 1991; Lincoln, 1991). Trito, a Indo-European warrior-hero whose name means "third," sets out to recover the tribe's cattle, which were taken by a three-headed monster. Usually this monster is symbolically aligned with members of cultures that are not Indo-European. Trito calls upon a warrior-god's aid and, through offering libations of intoxicating drinks, procures his support. Trito himself partakes of the intoxicants, rendering himself fearless, and with the help of the warrior-god defeats the monster and recovers the cattle.

Lincoln (1991) believes that this myth helped develop an accompanying ritual that placed within the social structure of the Indo-European warrior the expectation of stealing cattle. This included the priest of the tribe's symbolically reenacting the myth with the warriors, through ritual, before the latter went into battle. It also had implications for the initiation of young boys into the warrior status. The initiates would be instructed to engage in battle with a mock three-headed monster that resembled the one Trito had slain. This evoked powerful reactions in the young warriors, but, as Lincoln has noted, they soon came to see this effigy as one not to be feared and as undeserving of the cattle that were stolen. This instilled the attitude that those outside the tribe did not deserve such riches and were not to be feared.

One can also see the importance of the intoxicants among the later Indo-European descendants. Germanic/Nordic and Celtic peoples' warriors utilized illicit substances to induce the ferocious battle rage, or berserker state. The successful warrior then became a warrior-hero for his tribe; oftentimes the survival of the tribe depended upon acquiring economic sustenance or defeating what was perceived as a monster. The latter case, as Lincoln (1991) has noted, would include myths such as Saint Patrick's driving out the snakes from Ireland and Saint George's slaying the dragon. Examples of the cattle-saga motif in later Indo-European descendants include Hercules:

> In that season when Hercules bore off. . . . And himself being weary, he set down his cattle. . . . But they did not remain safe with Cacus ["the Evil One"], a faithless host: That one defiled Jove with theft. Cacus was an aborigine, a robber from a dread cave, who spoke through three separate mouths. He, in order that there be no clues to the theft, dragged the cattle backward into his cave—But not unwitnessed by the god. The young oxen betrayed the thief by their lowing, and the wrath pulled down the rough doors of the thief. Cacus lay dead, struck thrice by Hercules' club (Porpertius 4.9.1–20).

And then, in the Indian story of Trita:

> Trita, knowing the ancestral weapons and impelled by Indra [the warrior god], did battle. Having killed the three headed, seven-bridled one, Trita drove off his cattle. The mighty lord struck down that conceited one who had sought great power driving forth the cattle of Visvarupa, he tore off those three heads (Rig-Veda 10.8.8–9).

Both of these stories are derivatives of the ancient cattle cycle, discussed above.

In the story of the Irish hero Cuchuliann, there is also an emphasis placed upon protection of cattle. In fact, the Irish hero derives his name from this act. Given the name Setanta at birth, as a precocious child he was already showing signs of his heroic prowess. One evening, the Ulstermen were feasting at the house of Culann, who had a furious hound that protected the grounds and livestock. The boy Setanta, who had been forgotten during the feast, approached the grounds and was attacked by the hound. The Ulstermen were too afraid of the hound to assist the boy. The boy hurled a ball down the throat of the hound with such force that it came out its entrails. The Ulstermen rejoiced at the boy's strength and courage; all except Culann, who had lost his prized hound. Setanta then stated that he would act in the hound's stead, protecting the herds and the plains by himself. The Ulstermen named him *Cuchuliann*, which means "the hound of Culann." His role of protector is further amplified in the myth of the cattle raid, as he single-handedly protected the Ulster territory against four provinces of Ireland, slaying scores of men in the process.

CREATION MYTH AND THE KING

The cattle cycle is a part of the larger creation myth in the Indo-European legacy. In the beginning, there were two men—"man," who was the priest, and his brother "twin," who was the king (Lincoln, 1991; Mallory, 1991). They rode in a wagon drawn by an ox. One day, they decided they would create the world, and the priest offered up his brother, the king, and the ox as sacrifices to the gods. He then used the parts of the dismembered bodies to create the universe and human beings. From the king's body came the three differing classes of the culture. The roles of the priest and the king are firmly established in this myth of the first sacrifice.

The priestly role was to appease the sky god through ritual. This might include the offering of animal or human sacrifice in an attempt to gain the favor of the gods and thus procure more cattle. The celestial sovereigns would bestow cattle on the people, who would, in turn, lose them to the enemy by theft. The warrior class would recover them through raids and deliver the fair share to the priests, who would then make a sacrifice, thus delivering some of the cattle back to the deities in hopes that the gods would help them procure more cattle. These two differing functions were reflected and solidified in the two upper levels of the Indo-European culture—king/priest and warrior. This included the priest's providing justification to making holy war on those outside the tribe.

The role of the king also takes on symbolic meaning as the personification of caste within the tripartite society. As mentioned, the king is the culmination of the three functions and in theory is willing to give his life for those he represents. This role of the king is sacrifice for the preservation of the land and the people. The potential devastating disruption if these tasks are not handled properly can be seen in the vegetation god's annual death and resurrection. In the case of the vegetation god, who has his origin in the non-Indo-European, Eastern world, the male consort of the earth goddess would be sacrificed for the continued fecundity of the land and people. Winn (1995) has suggested that the Germanic peoples helped make the switch from the indigenous earth goddess to a male fertility symbol. However, the ancient Indo-European creation myth may suggest that the king already functioned to some extent in this capacity. Weston (1920/1993) has also argued that this theme can be seen in prehistory in the vegetation god rituals and the horse sacrifice myths and then, later, in the Middle Ages in the fisher king and grail myths. In the later grail legend, the fisher king receives a wound to the groin and is rendered physically and emotionally impotent. He occupies a place where he can neither live nor die. Because the land and the king are one, the kingdom suffers terribly until the secret of the grail is revealed and the king—and the land with him—is restored.

An example of this ritual symbolism is the horse sacrifice ceremony, which was seen as far east as India and as far west as Ireland. There is a recording of the ceremony in Ulster in 1185 C.E. A symbolic or substitute king was sacrificed in place of the actual leader. This ceremony was incorporated in the enthronement of the king, wherein a white mare was brought into the circle of the people (Sjoestedt, 1982). The soon-to-be-king approached the circle on all fours, declaring himself a beast. The mare was immediately sacrificed and dismembered, and a bath for the king was prepared from its boiling broth. The king was required to sit in the bath and lap up the broth. With these rites accomplished, his power and authority were ratified.

Lincoln (1991) has suggested that although the king came from the warrior class and went through elaborate ceremonies to confirm his kingship, he is not necessarily a warrior-king. Because the warrior class was seen as a necessary but dangerous element of society, the king needed to come from that class but perhaps also needed to keep some distance from it. In fact, Puhvel (1987) has proposed that the royal bloodline often strayed too far from the warrior ethic, and that the king was often in need of a true warrior as his mentor, consultant, or rescuer. Haudry (1999) has suggested that the king is the metaphoric "breastplate," "rampart," or "sentry of his people" (p. 54). While he does not do battle, he is essential to victory. Tacitus, in *Germania*, reports that the ancient Germans distinguished between kings and military chiefs. The former were chosen for their nobility and had the power to command, while the latter were chosen for valor and led by warrior example.

The king's function is also a political one, maintaining moral and social order. His function is to "stretch, draw out in a straight line, and straighten" (Mallory, 1991, p. 125). This is has been interpreted by some scholars as carrying out his kingly duties with outstretched arms and as being one who determines what is right. Haudry (1999) has suggested that the king is seen as the image of a straight path and thus as having a religious function. The king is closely aligned with the priestly function and in some instances, as with Celtic druids, with priests who were auxiliaries of the sacred kingship. In some cases, the priests are actually seen as occupying the topmost position, being superior even to the king. In the Indian ritual, the association between the king and his chief priest was celebrated as a wedding wherein the priest played the male, or dominate, role and the king, the subordinate, or feminine, one (Lincoln, 1991). However, when this balance of power occurs, it is often more a political/ideological smokescreen than a reality.

Further, the king is also the guarantor of prosperity for his people. There is an Indo-European metaphor of the king's being "the shepherd of his people" (this would take on a different meaning after the fusing of Indo-

European ideals with Christianity). The king leads his people to good grazing, an important ability for a nomadic herding culture. A good king from Homer's perspective, as demonstrated in the *Odyssey* is one "who, reigning in the fear of the gods over a large number of excellent men, remains true to justice, and the black earth bears him wheat and barley" (19.109). This quotation represents the king's duties to each of the three functions of the society over which he rules.

CONCLUSION

If we look at the Indo-European perspective as a foundation for Western masculinity, we can see that the first two castes (the king/priest and the warrior) have a special importance in the tripartite society. We shall refer to these as the "two masculinities" because they are the basis upon which the Indo-European masculine ideal is built. Aspects of each of these mythic frameworks will be revisited and reworked throughout our examination of Western masculinity.

In terms of the warrior's notion of a prototypical man, there is an emphasis upon fame and honor, which are achieved in part through lineage but also through one's own actions. The warrior is one who can ideally show courage, strength, and unflappability even when facing death or the disfavor of the gods. Individualism is personified in the PIE warrior as long as it stays within culturally accepted norms. This "shame culture" emphasizes a persona that is created and maintained in the public eye. To maintain that persona, bravado is a necessity, though one must be sure to back it up with deeds. There is also a cultural expectation that the warrior not cross the cultural taboo of "too much" aggression. When this occurs, the sins of the warrior may lead to his being ostracized within the community.

The king, on the other hand, is, in theory, the embodiment of all three functions of the culture. He is both political and spiritual and assumes responsibility for the fecundity of his land and the prosperity of his people. He acts as a moral guide, and, while coming from the warrior class or at least having some tie to it, he is often removed from the bellicosity of the warrior caste. The king must look to his warriors to fulfill this function for him. The king's function sets the mode for a ruling aristocracy, espousing more refinement than expected of warriors. This class distinction calls for differing codes of masculinity within the culture. While the warriors' task is to do the actual legwork of protecting and expanding the community, it is the king who directs them. He must walk a fine line between reining in the bellicosity of the warrior to maintain the continuation of the community and spurring it on when it is to the king-dom's advantage. Important aspects taken from each of these masculine prototypes will be recycled and renewed as we move through the subsequent examination of the cultural myth of masculinity.

While this book focuses primarily upon the first two castes of Indo-European culture, we must also consider the "third masculinity," that of the sustenance-provider caste in the Indo-European culture. Does this third caste have its own separate ideal of masculinity? If we view this caste as a later and somewhat foreign addition to the Indo-European culture as Dumézil's war of the functions suggests, then we would expect its members to have their own ideal that predates the joining of the two cultures. How much of this ideal survives past the joining of the Indo-European culture? Perhaps a concrete starting place for these answers is best found in the cultural tension seen in ancient Greek mythology.

As mentioned above, scholars suggest that the earth goddess culture eventually became the third caste in the Indo-European culture. In much of the mythology we have examined in this chapter, it appears as if there is an ancient version of the battle of the sexes wherein the men of the Indo-European culture are set against the women of the earth goddess culture. Scholars such as Eisler (1988) have interpreted the mythology as a duel between the two cultures as well as between the two genders. And yet, we should expect men of the earth goddess culture and notions of ideal masculinity to be involved in this process as well. We see that in these myths men of the earth goddess culture act in a distinctly non-Indo-European fashion. They have deep ties to the earth in their mythic symbolism. Further, they are given a monstrous persona by the Indo-European culture. This would suggest that the earth goddess culture had a masculine ideal and that it was distinctly different from the Indo-European one. The myth of Dionysus is a prime example.

In his original form, Dionysus may have represented the masculine ideal of the earth goddess culture. Scholars such as Highwater (1991) have suggested that his cultural roots are distinctly non-Indo-European. In later mythology, after the two cultures are joined, he occupies his Indo-European stepbrother Apollo's chair in his absence. This is quite an honor because Apollo is the Greek's ideal man. However, in Dionysus's original form, the Indo-Europeans viewed him in threatening terms. There are a number of reasons, among them his effeminate behavior; his special, reverent relationship with the women of his non-Indo-European culture; and his representing the ideal man of a foreign culture. In Greek cultural mythology, Dionysus is eventually revamped into a more Indo-European form. However, because of his original roots in a non-Indo-European culture, he is not ever given full membership in the pantheon on Olympus, though he is given special status as a son of Zeus.

If Dionysus does represent the masculine ideal of the earth goddess culture, did aspects of his original definition of masculinity survive through the joining of cultures and the development of the third Indo-European caste? By being connected to the fecundity of the earth, the ideal masculine characteristics of the earth goddess culture may have included many of the characteristics that the ancient Greeks labeled as belonging to their Indo-European women. A masculinity that is centered on those notions may have been dismissed in pejorative terms by the Indo-Europeans. Perhaps the battle of functions also held gender-role implications as the men of these differing cultures, with differing ideals of masculinity, were in competition for establishing the hegemonic model. Based on the fate of Dionysus, we see that the emphasis upon creative force was preserved but that much of what did not match the Indo-European ideal was altered.

Chapter 2

INDO-EUROPEAN HEROES AND ZANES

The concept of Indo-European heroes is well documented and denotes the individual who, through exemplary behavior, brings eternal fame to himself and/or to his people. Some writers have suggested that the profiles of heroes contain certain commonalties. For instance, there seem to be certain characteristics common to Indo-European heroes, including an unusual or miraculous birth, being part divine, and accomplishing a certain number of truly heroic accomplishments. However, we are most interested here in the hero's ability to both protect and expand his community. The hero undertakes feats both for his own glory (i.e., to achieve the fame that does not decay) and for the sake of his people. Both of these qualities are reflected in most Indo-European stories and are at the core of the Western masculine ethic. To knowingly undertake a task that may cost one's life is seen, in the Indo-European cultural myth of masculinity, as a fair trade-off if it will guarantee enduring fame and serve the community.

The other focus of this chapter is the exploration of zanes. The word *zane* originates with the ancient Greek Olympics and indicates a model of nonexemplary behavior. In the ancient Greek Olympics, honor and fair play were taken very seriously, so much so that each contestant had to swear an oath that he had trained hard and would not cheat. Those who broke their oath had statues made in their likeness (at their own expense) that were placed in the entry area of the games so that incoming athletes and spectators alike could take note of their dishonor.

Haudry (1999) has maintained that in Indo-European culture a particular import was placed upon public opinion as the criterion for personal worth. There is a strong indication that the culture was shame-based, and that respect for the moral code was maintained by the desire for praise and the fear of ridicule. To that end, heroes and zanes are a matched pair; in many myths, one becomes the foil for the other. These models become implicit and explicit examples of appropriate and inappropriate conduct within the context of the cultural myth. Both are important aspects of the socialization of men and the gender roles they are expected to assume.

In our exploration of the hero there are two differing approaches. First, definitions of heroes and zanes can be viewed through the contextual lens of history, culture, social class, and the hegemonic model of masculinity. For instance, the medieval tales of the hero Robin Hood resonate with an aristocracy that is chastised in the tale for class distinction without care for those below them on the socioeconomic ladder. If looked at from Dumézil's model of a tripartite Indo-European culture (1970, 1973), there are multiple levels of consideration. There is the failure of the king, who is supposed to embody all three functions of the culture, that is, aristocracy, warrior, and sustenance provider. The failure occurs on two levels. One belongs to King Richard the Lion-Hearted, for leaving his people unattended as he goes to the Crusades. The other failure occurs as the shady prince John fills his brother's place. Under John's rule the third function is particularly abused. In order to right this wrong, the rebel aristocrat/warrior Robin Hood robs from the rich and gives to the poor. Members of the third level of society who live in the forest unite with Robin Hood in order to set right the wrongs perpetrated by John. In the end Richard returns from the Crusades, resumes his hero status, and deposes John. The Robin Hood myth provides a contextual model for cultural order and right-doing on the part of the nobility and gives examples of potential heroes to emulate.

The second approach to examining the hero myth is to explore specific stories of heroes that have been sustained over time. This is not an exploration of the specific sociocultural forces that helped create these heroic tales, but rather it represents a broader reflection of a hegemonic masculinity. For instance, heroes such as King Arthur, Hercules, and Beowulf speak to models of masculinity that strike a particular chord in Western culture. This second approach points us to descriptive models that have a sustained popularity and have been recycled time and again. This broader-stroke approach is the one most employed in this chapter. The heroes and zanes discussed here are ones who have survived the test of time because they seem to resonate with ongoing notions of the cultural myth of masculinity. However, we must first consider some of the mythologists' and writers' notions of the hero than can be adapted to our examination of the Indo-European hero.

HEROES

Many authors have contributed to the analysis of the hero themes in Western myth. Among the more prominent contributors have been psychoanalysts Otto Rank and Carl Jung and mythologists Joseph Campbell and Lord Fitzroy Richard Raglan. Each of these theorists has added differing perspectives to the mythic theme in question. The commonalties of the hero versions they have identified are the struggles, hardships, and/or adventures the hero must endure. There is something heroic in what the hero does in that it is outside the realm of normal functioning or existence. The journey can be an external one, as in the cases discussed by Rank and Raglan wherein kingdoms are won and/or monsters and villains slain. It may also be an internal one, as in the cases discussed by Jung and Campbell wherein wisdom is obtained through the hero's journey. In both types of example, something is gained for the individual and/or the community through the heroic action. Each of the above theorists brings a different perspective to our understanding of the Indo-European hero.

OTTO RANK

Otto Rank wrote *The Myth of the Birth of Hero* (1914/1959) while still a devoted disciple of Freud. Therefore, it should come as no surprise that his discussions of heroic journeys have much to do with Oedipal fantasies and conflicts. For Rank, all the important symbols in the tales were disguised aspects of the Oedipal myth. His notion of the hero was in keeping with Freud's conception of a sublimated fantasy of conquering the father and marrying the mother. The hero's actions are directed toward this aim, to defeat those who would block him from the tender devotion of his mother (symbolically or literally). The hero becomes heroic because he dares to challenge his father's place beside his mother. However, for most normal people this truth is too horrendous to face. Therefore the mythic tale is devised (or created) so as to disguise the hero's incestuous wish as a striving for power through defeating his father. Of course, the perfect example of this hero pattern is Oedipus himself. The hero rises from obscurity after being abandoned or rejected by his parents, especially his father.

Rank has suggested, in keeping with Freud, that there is a certain class of individuals called psychoneurotics who, though mature physically, remain psychological and emotional children. For them it is too threatening to verbalize their unconscious Oedipal fantasies. From Rank's perspective, these neurotic individuals read the hero myth and, by doing so, vicariously live out the Oedipal wish. Given the unconscious desire and the magic of wish fulfillment obtained through reading the myth, it is the best compromise at which they can arrive.

LORD RAGLAN

In Lord Raglan's work *The Hero: A Study in Tradition, Myth, and Drama* (1956), the mythologist develops a detailed point system with which he examines numerous mythic heroes, noting their commonalties. These range from royal birth to living in exile to a later triumphant return to finally obtaining a kingship and eventually being sacrificed (literally or figuratively) for the continuation or replenishment of the community. Raglan rates each hero as to how well his life adhered to the twenty-two-point system. His ratings include Oedipus, who receives a perfect score, and Dionysus and King Arthur, who each received scores of nineteen.

Raglan's hero follows a prescribed pattern of action. Though the would-be hero faces many hardships and difficulties, he becomes king and reigns in this position for some time. The saga culminates with his experiencing a decline as ruler and, eventually, death. While triumphing over adversity, the hero/king's ultimate heroic action is not the slaying of monsters or vanquishing of foes, but rather his own death, through which he secures the continuation of the kingdom at his own expense.

Raglan has suggested that this is because myth and ritual are closely intertwined. In the case of the king, he argues that the ultimate aim is to relive the ancient cycle of the vegetation god in the guise of the king. In the vegetation god myth, there is a pattern of the birth, growth, death, and eventual return of the male vegetation god, which allows for continued renewal of the kingdom's resources. The king's ritual of the death and resurrection of the vegetation god leads to the regeneration of the land. The land and the king are intertwined in an ongoing cycle of birth, death, and renewal. A strong king will lead to abundant resources within the kingdom. However, as his fecundity begins to wane, so too will the kingdom begin to suffer. To this end, there must be a renewal of the vegetation god's presence in the symbolic removal of the king. The king must die and be replaced by a more vital force—a new hero who will become king.

This closely intertwined aspect of myth/ritual follows James Frazer's (1922) second law of magic seen in primitive societies, wherein the imitation of what one wants to happen may cause the actual event to occur. Therefore, to act out a ritual is to bring its power or meaning to life. In this case, the revitalization of the land is accompanied through acting out the vegetation cycle by portraying the death (symbolic or literal) of the king. The vegetation god is best exemplified in the story of Dionysus, the god of the vine, wherein there is a seasonally based birth, growth, death, and resurrection.

CARL JUNG AND JOSEPH CAMPBELL

Carl Jung (1956) and Joseph Campbell (1956) have similar views of heroes. Both focus on the journey into the internal world. The hero is heroic because he is not only able to separate emotionally from his parents and renounce his antisocial inclinations (both tasks of the first half of life), but he is also able to move from the unconscious realm of existence. This is accomplished through the hero's going off to a strange land where he encounters male and female deities. They are not his parents, and neither are they a couple. Generally, he marries the female god and kills and eats the male one. In this way the hero gains a sense of mystical union with both gods. It is through this mystical union that he more fully develops his psyche, thus gaining secret wisdom. Having gone through the mystical initiation by embarking upon this journey, the hero, Jung argues, must leave this new world and return to the old in order to save his community. For Jung, the hero comes home humbled and has attained a new sense of wisdom that he will in turn impart to his community in an altruistic fashion. For Campbell, the hero not only returns to the old world but also sees it with fresh eyes as a result of his transformation. Campbell's hero comes home to assume an exalted place in his society.

THE HERO

Campbell's, Jung's, and Raglan's heroes intersect in at least one important way—each hero undergoes the journey for the betterment or survival of the community—sometimes wittingly, sometimes unwittingly (Segal, 1990). For Campbell and Jung, the hero expands the community, and for Raglan, he guarantees its continuation through self-sacrifice. From the perspective of these important works, the hero does what he does in part for the betterment of the community. There is great praise for the hero who can expand the wealth, property, boundaries, and survival of the community at the risk of his own life. Indeed, this is reflected in the Indo-European cattle saga, as well as in the story of the king embodying the three functions of the culture. This dynamic is also seen in the case of Beowulf: The hero journeys to another land to help friendly allies rid themselves of their problem. After twelve seasons of having their great hall violated nightly by the monster Grendel, Beowulf arrives to relieve the situation. Through brute strength he rips the shoulder and connected arm from Grendel. Later he swims to the bottom of the lake to do battle with Grendel's mother, whom he beheads. Beowulf makes the great hall safe again for the community. He will, in his latter years, when he becomes ruler of his own land, do battle with and triumph over a dragon at the cost of his own life. Again, we see the same theme: The hero protects the community.

There is another aspect to consider, however: the hero's undertaking is his journey for his own gain. This is consistent with Rank's view of the hero. It is difficult to know the personal motives of the ancient hero, but we can infer greed, power, and—perhaps above all—glory. As previously mentioned, Lincoln (1991) describes the latter as the striving for "the fame that does not decay." Indeed, in a precarious world where a life could be easily extinguished and perhaps just as easily forgotten, the idea of obtaining a sense of immortality through heroic deeds must have been very appealing. We see it in the Irish myth of Cuchuliann, when Cathbad was instructing his hundred pupils and was asked about the virtue of the day. He said that whoever took up arms on that day would live a glorious but short life. The boy warrior Cuchuliann gladly made the choice.

In Nordic myth, a proud warrior death not only guarantees a place in the warriors' hall of Valhalla, it can also possibly secure lasting fame if one's deeds were heroic enough to repeat in the great hall. We even can identify this theme in Shakespeare's *Henry V*. Henry and his troops, severely outnumbered, face almost certain death against the French. Henry's famous St. Crispin's Day speech rallies the troops as he declares that other men in years to come "will count their manhood cheap" (1988 version, 4.3.68) because they were not there on that day to fight and possibly die with such honor.

Honor and fame are at the heart of the hero. His actions and thoughts are geared toward both. We will see that in the transformation of the Indo-European warrior to the Christian knight, the seat of fame and honor is changed. In the earlier manifestation the warrior is the recipient of both. It is through his *arte*, or striving for perfection, that his great feats are accomplished. But in the case of the medieval knight, those who are worthy do more. The fame and praise of the humble knight belongs to God.

It is through purity and alignment with God that the Christian knight conquers. The more worthy knight will always triumph over the false one; God has ordained it so.

ZANES

Zanes, the statue likenesses of ancient Greek Olympic athletes who cheated in their training or when competing, can be viewed as the foils for heroes. They are the antithesis of the dominant prototype of a culture's definition of masculinity. Zane characteristics include cheating to try to win a battle, boasting of strength or heroic feats without having the capacity to back it up, and acting in an otherwise dishonorable fashion. Two categories of zanes are examined here: (1) those who act as a foil for the hero; and (2) the hero who becomes a zane but somehow redeems himself.

Indo-European myth is full of zanes of the first variety. In fact, it is difficult to have the hero establish his valor without having a foil against whom to compete. For instance, we see in the cattle raid myth of Cuchuliann those who would boast of their strength, prowess, and ability only to be easily defeated in battle later. The Irish hero spends much of the tale defeating such characters. In the same fashion, Beowulf encounters a contemporary who, unlike the others, is not impressed by the hero's nobility, courage, and other heroic characteristics. He attempts to mock Beowulf. However, when push comes to shove, this would-be hero also comes to shame as Beowulf undoes him in both word and deed. In these situations the zane does not equal the hero in prowess and skill.

We see in some versions of the Arthurian tales that the foil is Arthur's own son, Mordrid. As Mordrid attempts a campaign of corruption against Camelot, a final battle ensues in which he and Arthur face each other. Feigning a desire for reconciliation, Mordrid mortally wounds Arthur, and Arthur in turn delivers the deathblow to his son. Mordrid represents a special quality of some zanes, in that challenging the hero directly will leave the zane mismatched in skill and valor. It is only through dishonest means or trickery that the hero can be undone.

There are other cases wherein the zane and the hero are more equally matched, and it is the heroic essence that will make the difference in the final battle. We see this theme recycled in more contemporary classics as well, such as in Owen Wister's *The Virginian*. This book represents the heroic virtue in cowboy form. His foil is another cowboy who matches the hero in skill and prowess. In fact, early on the foil cowboy betters the Virginian in a game of cards and calls him a "son of a bitch," thus insulting his honor. The famous line follows: "When you call me that, smile." In the final showdown it is touch and go as to who will emerge victorious.

In terms of the second type of zane, the hero gone awry, there are also prominent examples in Indo-European myth. In this case, the hero, having already earned his status, will spoil his accomplishments and act in the way of a zane through committing the sins of the warrior (Dumézil, 1970). In most cases the hero is given an opportunity to redeem himself and return to his former status. Three prominent myths wherein this occurs include those of Hercules, Achilles, and Lancelot.

Hercules, a son of Zeus with amazing strength and the potential to be a hero, is caught in an ongoing battle with Hera, Zeus's wife. On a surface level there is animosity because Hercules is the product of yet another one of Zeus's numerous affairs. As mentioned earlier, on a cultural level this reflects the tension of the clash between Indo-European and pre-Greek cultures. In any case, Hera at every turn tries to sabotage Hercules as the hero. This occurs throughout his life as he does battle with a number of monsters under Hera's influence. The irony is that the name *Hercules* actually means "glory of Hera." However, her glory in the conflict is diminished as Hercules grows in fame for defeating titans and monsters at Hera's expense.

Hera does succeed in one episode of the saga, as she causes Hercules to go mad. He goes into a battle rage and mistakenly kills his wife and children. At this point the mighty hero obtains zane status. He is the antithesis of the hero. However, he is given the opportunity to redeem himself through the twelve labors, which he eventually completes. In some tales Hercules is even invited by Hera to join the gods on Olympus.

Lancelot of the lake is not so fortunate. As the champion of Camelot and best friend to King Arthur, he accomplishes much. He is the knightly ideal in battle as well as in the court of chivalry. However, his affair with Arthur's wife, Guinevere, brings him down to zane status. Lancelot eventually lives in the wilderness as a monk trying to redeem himself for his actions. However, though he attempts penance, Lancelot has an incomplete personal redemption, finding peace instead through his son Galahad. Galahad is the chaste, pure knight who will be one of a very few who learn the secret of the Holy Grail. While in some versions Lancelot after his penitence is given a glimpse of the grail's secret, his exposure to its rapture ends his life.

Finally, mighty Achilles is the warrior who brings his prowess to bear in Homer's *Iliad*. He is the champion of the Greeks who besiege Troy for ten years. In Book 24 of the *Iliad*, Achilles, grown weary of combat and feeling slighted by his fellow Greeks, withdraws from battle. This places the Greek forces in danger. The generals attempt to persuade him to rejoin the battle before all is lost, but to no avail. His best comrade, Patroklos, seeing the plight of the Greek army, asks if he can put on the hero's armor and masquerade as him in order to rally the troops. Achilles consents to the ploy. His comrade puts on the armor, goes to battle, and is mortally wounded by the Trojan hero Hector. Achilles, hearing the news of his friend and feeling shamed for his less-than-heroic behavior, resumes the battle and eventually does single combat with Hector. When Achilles prevails, he drags the dead body of his foe behind his chariot as he circles the walls of Troy.

Achilles' unwillingness to resume battle, allowing his friend to die in his stead, and—perhaps worst of all—dishonoring the dead, place him in zane status. Achilles' redemption comes through Hector's father, Priam. This old man puts on a disguise and comes into Achilles' tent at the risk of his own life. He begs for the body of his son for proper funeral rites. The conversation between the two is among the most moving in literature. Priam reminds Achilles of his own bond with his father, who has passed away. The encounter ends when both warriors become tearful for their losses and Achilles relents.

CONCLUSION

Heroes and zanes are interrelated concepts that serve the function of providing cultural icons and codes of appropriate behavior for men. By examining the paired heroes and zanes, it can be seen in one fell swoop which masculine virtues are idealized and which are held in contempt. Of course, this analysis is subject to contextual examination, and as one would expect, these myths' icons and definitions are in accordance with the hegemonic masculinity of their time. Moreover, just as the concept of the hegemonic masculinity changes, so does the definition of what constitutes heroic masculinity. Each may have some permeability over time. For example, we will see in the next chapter, when discussing chivalry, that there are competing models for the aristocratic warrior and some confusion over which is the hero and which is the zane. Is the zane the one who emulates the old hardened-warrior ethic of the Indo-European world, or the courtly gentleman who, in juxtaposition, curls his hair, wears fancy adornment, and acts in more refined ways?

Our examination in this chapter primarily focused upon a second method for studying the hero myth as a model of potential masculinity. We examined with broad strokes the hero and zane icons who have survived over time. The examination of the various notions of the hero taken from mythologists and psychoanalysts such as Jung, Campbell, Raglan, and Rank reveals that, ultimately, the hero serves two functions in the Indo-European community: (1) to bring everlasting fame to himself, and (2) to enrich or sustain the community. These two functions are often intertwined in the stories and provide the substance of what is valued as heroic in the culture.

We must also consider social class in our examination of the hero as the ultimate masculine ideal in Western culture. The social lineage of the hero is found in the first two castes of the Indo-European culture. Although he may often mistakenly begin life as a member of the third caste, or sustenance providers (e.g., farmers, herders, workers), he invariably transcends that caste to take his rightful place, often first as hero then later as king. It is his true noble or warrior spirit that allows him to transcend caste as well as to accomplish the heroic task at hand. There is a strong mythos that a commoner remains in the third caste but that something special about the hero allows him to transcend it. This speaks to the cultural belief that the first two castes—aristocracy and warrior—are valued the most, while the third caste is often seen as a marker of lower living. This has direct implications for a potentially pejorative attitude toward the masculine definitions and ideals of the third caste. Much of the heroic mythos suggests that true heroes cannot really come from this social class. If they do, as in the case of the Robin Hood myth (i.e., many of the "merry men" are members of the third caste) they are in the service of the more accepted version of the hero. Like the merry men, they may perform some heroic actions, but they play an auxiliary role because their main purpose is to bring fame to the hero. It is only the later birth of the middle class, with its militarization of masculinity, that allows this to change.

Chapter 3

CHIVALRY

Chivalry is a concept that carries many associations. In its strictest sense, it is the code of conduct associated with the arms-bearing aristocracy of the Middle Ages. It is an oftentimes romanticized notion of saving damsels in distress, righting wrongs, and acting to serve one's king, all while following the ways of the Christian God. Aspects of chivalry also have come to be associated with the knight-errant aspect of seeking adventure and being on a quest. It is this aspect of chivalry that may lay at the foundation of colonization. Later, we can see this fluid concept evolving to accommodate the persona of the cowboy who saves the town from wrongdoers or even the "knights of the air" who flew World War I combat missions in their planes. To speak of chivalry, then, is to allude to a gamut of ideas related, at least in theory, to noble acts of masculinity. These acts will vary, of course, depending upon the time period and culture. This chapter is devoted to the examination of the foundations of chivalry, its subsequent evolutions, and how these have had an impact upon the masculine ideals that chivalry sets forth.

ROOTS OF CHIVALRY

Keen (1984) argued that the roots of chivalry lie in blending of Teutonic warrior and aristocracy beliefs with the Judeo-Christian tradition. This is taken a step further here, in that Teutonic ideals are actually Indo-European ones. This synthesis of paradigms leads to a new cultural dynamic. With that said, there has always been an uneasy tension between the militant role of the warrior and the pacifist stance of the church. This can be seen in the precursor Hebrew tradition wherein the Hebrew Bible reveals Jehovah at times as the god of vengeance. Abraham, Moses, and Lot all speak on behalf of their own peoples and others, pleading to God to show mercy. Then there are warriors such as Joshua, David, and Judea Maccabees (whose name literally means "one who strikes"), who conquered in a ferocious manner. In contrast, later prophets such as Isaiah tell us to beat our swords into plowshares, and the New Testament's Prince of Peace says the meek will inherit the earth, with the greatest commandment being, love thy neighbor.

In any case, after the conversion of Constantine to Christianity and the creation of the Holy Roman Empire in 800 C.E., it fell upon the Christian emperor to defend Christendom. Later, in the ninth century, Carolingian Europe experienced invasions from all sides, including attacks perpetrated by Vikings and Hungarians. Again the church was forced to come to grips with the importance of the military role in protecting the Christian kingdoms and the church. Augustine's fourth-century philosophy of the "just war" placed this ongoing philosophical tension in perspective. Militant force could be used to right a wrong when the wrong-doing party deliberately breached the peace and would not make reparations. Force could also be used to bring sinners back into the fold. This, of course, would later help build the case for using deadly force to convert heretics and unbelievers.

This uneasy alliance between bellicosity and peace helped set the stage for chivalry's development (Keen, 1984). Pope Leo IV appealed for support in 853 C.E. when the Saracens were threatening Rome: "He who dies in battle will not be denied the heavenly kingdom, for the Almighty will know that he died for the truth of our faith . . . and the defense [of Christianity]." Pope Urban II's crusading appeal in 1095 C.E. led to the development of the idea that being a knight was a Christian vocation: "Let those who were robbers now be the soldiers of Christ . . . let those who have been hirelings for a few pieces of silver attain an eternal reward" (Keen, 1984, p. 48).

The use of the Crusade was a remarkable way to blend military force with a Christian mission (Keen, 1984). The launching of the Crusades was a decisive point in the development of chivalry. The secular qualities that marked the older Nordic/Germanic hero, such as loyalty and honor, helped establish stereotypes of chivalric behavior. There were already marks of the hero in the older Indo-European literature that predated Christianity. For instance, in the Anglo-Saxon epic *Beowulf*, youth is seen as a testing time when a young warrior in the service of a foreign lord makes a name for himself. He then returns triumphantly as a hero. Still earlier, we see the Greek hero going off to the wilderness on a sojourn. These events would set the literary stage for the later myths of the knight-errant in the Arthurian tradition. The underlying common theme to the Greek hero, Beowulf, and the crusaders was that all fought perceived monsters, be they deputies of the mother goddess, Grendel, or the Saracens. This model is in keeping with the Indo-European tradition of seeing enemies as monsters who hold possessions that they do not rightly deserve.

In addition, the Crusades provided an opportunity to incorporate the Indo-European hero myth and place it within the context of Christianity. Young knights had the opportunity to prove themselves in a foreign land, returning as triumphant heroes. All the while, the Christian church sanctioned their bellicosity and taking of lives. These heroes and those who died in battle obtained the twin goals of living a chivalrous life in this world—fulfilling the Indo-European need for honor and glory, the fame that does not decay (Lincoln, 1991)—and at the same time gaining eternal salvation in the next.

The dual theme of adventure and exploration is deeply embedded within chivalry. This has its roots in the ethic of the Indo-European warrior and is brought forward in the chivalry system by the veneration of the crusading knight and the knight-errant. The story of the Holy Grail highlights the importance of exploration for the chivalrous knight. When each knight left the Round Table in pursuit of the Grail, he chose to go on pathways that were unknown. It was a disgrace for a knight to follow in the tracks of another rather than plot his own course. Mythologist Joseph Campbell (1956) has interpreted this myth as furthering the definition of Western individualism.

In addition, the later development of nineteenth-century sexology and psychoanalysis paradigms viewed the concept of the hero's proving himself as providing the middle-class model for the development of proper young men. The same theme of the boy's need to break free from the safety of the maternal relationship and explore the world independently was seen to be a part of the correct development of masculinity. When the boy had proven himself in the world, he might then return a hero, and only then might he move into an opposite-sex romantic relationship.

CHIVALRIC MYTH

In Maurice Keen's examination of chivalry (1984), he argues that medieval writers drew heavily upon myths from antiquity as models for their new warrior knights. Keen also suggests that writers of the era retrospectively examined myths of antiquity from the perspective and through the biased lens of their day.

> The attitudes thus exemplified are not those of the classical age, but are medieval, and they become typical in all manner of romances of the later twelfth and thirteenth centuries, not just those dealing with the classical past. (p. 110)

As a case in point, medieval writers argued the existence of medieval notions of chivalry in the heroes and tales of antiquity. For example, J. Monfrin wrote of ancient Rome:

> Considering that the Roman people, among all others, by the virtues of constancy and prudence and by their chivalrous deeds . . . knew how to achieve so much that by their wisdom and labor they conquered the whole world, we may see that every ruler may take example from their wonderful deeds. (cited in Keen, 1984, p. 111)

In *Romance of Alexander,* we see Alexander the Great and his young companions bathing themselves before taking the rites of knighthood. They also receive praise for the knightly qualities they possess, which include the protection of orphans and widows. Alexander's companions number twelve, a parallel to Charlemagne's paladins.

In *Christine de Pizan's Letter of Othea to Hector,* Perseus's rescue of Andromeda teaches knights to rescue those ladies in need of rescuing. Perseus's winged horse, Pegasus, signifies that a knight's good name should be spread throughout all countries. This certainly seems to echo, now with a more chivalrous twist, the Indo-European theme of seeking the fame that does not decay.

Part of this Medieval focus was to connect the present-day rulers to those of antiquity (remember the importance of lineage in the Indo-European culture, mentioned in chapter 1). To that end, impressive pedigrees were contrived that linked rulers to Roman, Celtic, and Judeo-Christian heroes and their myths. Geoffrey of Monmouth's tales (1997 version) of Arthur and his knights are full of references to the Roman poet Virgil and even trace the lineage of Arthur to Brutus, the first king of Britain, and ultimately to Aeneas, the Trojan hero. Indeed, the Franks even traced their lineage back to Hector of Troy. The irony of this lies in how the myth of the *Iliad* has been cycled and recycled. For the ancient Greeks, Homer's tale of the siege of Troy integrated and solidified their mythology and their mythological bloodline. It was some 500 years later that Virgil, wanting to appease Augustus Caesar and give the Roman bloodline an impressive pedigree, revised the same tale. In this newer version, Virgil explained away the Greek victory through sneaky and cowardly means (the Trojan horse) and claimed that the Roman lineage could be drawn from the noble Trojans who fought bravely to their deaths. Aeneas, who in Homer's version of the *Iliad* was a Trojan coward who escaped the Greek sword, becomes, in Virgil's version, the progenitor of the noble line through which Rome could be traced. Nearly a thousand years later, in medieval times, we see the tale being recycled yet again, this time making the Franks (Charlemagne and Arthur) the direct descendants of Rome and Aeneas. Making a Frank of Arthur is, of course, a historical blunder because many historians claim he was a Roman soldier who stayed behind on Britain after the withdrawal of Roman forces from the island. In either case, myth again is more about a paradigm of reality than about reality itself. Thus medieval writers took full poetic license when using ancient myths to complete their new model for the masculine paradigm.

Keen (1984) also has argued for the influence of the Judeo-Christian paradigm in the making of the code of chivalry. This is a most important grafting onto the Indo-European tradition. A Hebrew, non-Indo-European mythology of love, forgiveness, and being in a relationship with a single God fused with the tradition of a pantheon of gods that have mortal flaws of passion, lust, and greed. As the Christian myth borrowed from the Hebrew paradigm (which was itself influenced by the Greeks), we see how this potent synthesis ultimately guided the Holy Roman Empire. This Western/Christian approach comprises a mythological paradigm synthesizing Indo-European, old-world European, Semitic, Christian, and Greek beliefs. The wellspring of chivalry came from this complex mix. It took the Indo-European warrior and gave him an injection of love, gentleness, and mercy. Honor, duty, and loyalty were already a part of the Indo-European warrior tradition, but in the new paradigm there was a strong motivation to incorporate more refined aspects that were culturally connected to a striving for godliness or, at least, to service as a part of one's Christian duty.

To this end, Old Testament leaders were recycled and fashioned into models of knightly and Christian virtue. A list would include David, Joshua, Judea Maccabees, and Gideon. Again, medieval writers looked backward to confirm the longstanding existence of a recently created paradigm. It seemed especially appropriate that warriors of the Old Testament, who defended the Holy Land against the infidels, would be viewed as being strikingly parallel to the knight in the age of the Crusades (Keen, 1984). Crusaders who walked the same land and defended the perceived same honor of God as did their Old Testament predecessors seemed to draw strength and inspiration from those who went before them. When Lancelot asked the Lady of the Lake if there was any knight who carried all the virtuous points of chivalry before, she answered that Judas Maccabees, King David, and Joseph of Arimathea were fine examples.

The latter example was especially important for the fusion of the Christian paradigm with that of the Indo-European line. Joseph of Arimathea was the man who collected the body of Christ and stored his blood in a chalice (which had been used at the Last Supper). When the tale of Joseph of Arimathea was intermingled with the chalice symbol in Celtic myth, the result would become the Holy Grail of the Arthurian legend. Arthur and Christ are further linked as the ultimate aim of the knights of the Round Table was the quest for this Holy Grail and its power to spiritually and physically resurrect the land and the king. Further, Galahad, to whom the secret of the Grail was fully revealed, traced his bloodline to King David and to Joseph. This was in keeping with the Jewish tradition that the Messiah would come from the line of David and the Christian one that Jesus was the Messiah.

In keeping with the idea that chivalry and its impact on the masculine role in Western society were formed from the grafting of Old Testament influence and Christian myths, Jean de Longuyon, a fourteenth-century writer, introduced the "nine worthies." This is a collection of the nine best examples of chivalry—three from the world of antiquity, three from the Old Testament, and three from Christianity. They included Hector, Alexander, and Julius Caesar; Joshua, David, and Judas Maccabees; and Arthur, Charlemagne, and Godfrey of Bouillon. Of these, the final worthy may be the least recognized. He was the knight who freed Jerusalem for a short time from the infidels. Keen (1984) points out that Godfrey was by far the most recent edition to the chivalrous pantheon, carrying the implied message that chivalry and its message were ongoing even into the fourteenth century. It also suggested that there might be room for still-newer inductions into the chivalrous tradition if a man proved his worth. For instance, some made arguments for Robert the Bruce, who freed Scotland from England, as the tenth worthy.

COURTLY REVISIONS OF MASCULINITY

At the end of the tenth and the beginning of the eleventh centuries, southern France saw a long period of peace and prosperity that is believed to have set the ground for the growth of courtly ways (Jaeger, 1985). Courtliness was well in place by the twelfth century, having spread across Europe like wildfire. This phenomenon saw the transformation of the evolving Indo-European warrior into the chivalrous knight, who is supposed to emulate the courtly lifestyle. The "natural ethic," which is ultimately borrowed from the Greek belief that beauty is virtue, was revamped in the Middle Ages. The external refinements of the male nobility reflected the well-ordered inner harmony of the individual. Some gentry did interpret this as justification for the men's new fashion, emphasizing the beauty of the body as exemplified by contouring tight tunics, eye-catching adornments, plucked eyebrows, smooth faces, long curly hair (created by the use of hot irons), and curved shoes. This new ethic also stressed the use of courtly ways in the areas of proper eating, speaking, and walking. Some opponents of this new ethic saw this as the softening of the male warrior/aristocracy, while others within that same caste interpreted it as a sign of their cultural superiority over those they ruled (Keiser, 1997). Further, as courtly love evolved, there also arose a tension between the battled-hardened warrior of the ancient ways who cherished honor and loyalty and the knight who, while still serving as a retainer for his lord, subordinated himself to the love of the courtly lady. His striving for the love of women shaped the knight in ways that caused him to assume softer and stereotypically feminine ways (Keiser, 1997).

This new evolution was not without its critics. Leading the charge against this trend was the conservative clergy, who needed hardened warriors as protectors of Christendom. They saw a lasting peace as the breeding ground for a lazy, slack nobility whose job should be militant in the church's service. Courtly ways were seen as softening the warrior whose testing ground was the field of battle. This is echoed in the scene from Geoffrey of Monmouth's *Historia Regum Britanniae*, in which the procurator of Rome challenges King Arthur's court to battle. Duke Cador of Cornwall declares:

> Up to now I have been in fear lest the leisure which the Britons have enjoyed because of the long peace should render them listless and cowardly, destroying the fame of their deeds of war. . . . Where the exercise of arms is seen to make way to the allurements of dicing and women and other pleasures, it is inevitable that the reputation for strength, honor, and daring is tainted by the reproach of cowardice . . . God has stirred up the Romans against us, so that they may restore our prowess to what it was in the old days. (p. 248)

Another protester against this transformation was the cleric Saxo Grammaticus. Writing around the twelfth century, he was known for creating a pseudohistory based upon pagan tales. He told the story of Starcatherus, a Danish ancient hero who was the antithesis of this new, softened warrior: Starcatherus is ugly, old, dressed in rags, and satisfied with rancid meat. He is both treacherous and murderous. The hero visits the Danish court, where traditional heroic ideals have been replaced by courtly lavishness. Starcatherus seeks out Ingellus, the debonair Danish king, to set things right, but before the king recognizes the old hero he is mistreated and mistaken for a beggar by courtiers and the king's own wife. Upon recognizing Starcatherus, the king rebukes all those who offended the old hero, including the queen. She attempts to make amends to the hero through gifts that he throws back at her. Starcatherus makes a long speech bemoaning the new ways and criticizing Ingellus for his lack of manly virtue. The king is so shamed and moved by the speech that he takes his sword and kills all the corrupting Saxons at his table (Jaeger, 1985).

The French *La Mort le Roi Artu* (The Death of King Arthur) also reveals the climate of the times (T. Mallory, 1972 version). Arthur, Lancelot, and Gawain are old men who are no longer impervious to wounds in battle and unable to revive the vigor of their youth. We are told that there has not been an adventure in the realm in twenty years. The implication is that peace is a corrupting force to the spirit of the knight.

As late as the fourteenth century, the story of Sir Gawain and the Green Knight showcases the overornamented world of Camelot, contrasting its courtly ways to those of the old warriors' ethic. The queen is decked in ornate fabric and jewels; there is a focus on courtly feasting that is symbolic of the new order of civilization. Hanning (1972) has noted that in this new Arthurian world, the emphasis upon aesthetics is equal to if not greater than on the heroic. This is an important development in the definition of the warrior persona. Jaeger (1985) distinguishes the code of courtly ethics, wherein there is an emphasis upon more humane forms of relating, from the social order of the court, wherein fashion and excess are the norm. Saxo Grammaticus does not criticize the former but only the latter, when it portrays men as being overly effeminate (by the standards of the day). In many ways, the gift of chivalry in the guise of courtly ways allows for more civilized manners of behaving. Arthur, who was long held up as the ultimate mentor of young men, allows for warrior masculinity that can at the same time be relational in stance. That is, room is made for humanity amidst the bellicosity. This model veers into trouble only when, as is the case of Starcatherus and Ingellus, it leans too far in degrading aspects of the warrior that have been long-held as heroic.

THE END OF CHIVALRY

Several new fifteenth-century developments lead to the end of chivalry proper. Keen (1984) has argued that these included a more effective taxation system that made standing armies more possible. Before the existence of standing armies, the nobles would call upon their retainer knights to protect the providence. With the rise of standing armies, providence enjoyed year-round protection and service. This impacted the aristocracy of the knights whose old duties (at least according to the myth) were to follow the chivalrous code of protecting the weak and orphaned. Now, officers who commanded subunits of armies donned uniforms to distinguish themselves from the enemy. Furthermore, with the introduction and acceptance of handguns, the way that the warrior fought was changed. Sir Thomas Mallory (ca. 1405–71) could adapt the myth of Arthur and Charlemagne to his times, but subsequent writers had more difficulty doing so once the lance, jousting, and full body armor were fading in popularity. However, the underlying themes of honor, nobility, courage, and loyalty were retained. With or without the armor, these themes would endure.

CONCLUSION

In the medieval period class definitions of masculinity seem to collide. In chapter 1 we saw that the warrior class and the ruling aristocracy had differing functions and, with them, potentially differing definitions of prototypical masculinity. In the Middle Ages these varied definitions of masculinity became much more pronounced and differentiated. We saw that men of the Middle Ages were presented with the task of attempting to blend together more polarized versions of the two former Indo-European paradigms of masculinity. For instance, should men follow the hardened notions of the warrior class or the ever-more-refined ways of the ruling nobility? Difficult questions such as this placed men who were in the position to potentially straddle both worlds in an untenable position. The cultural dialectic brought to bear competing definitions of masculinity. This seemed to cause role confusion for men of this period. This tension and attempts to resolve it are reflected at the cultural level through the myths and stories of the time. The differing camps seemed poised to do battle for the claim of being the dominant masculine prototype. Though the myths of this period attempted to work out this cultural dynamic, a suitable solution was not found, other than to reinforce the already existing dichotomized versions of masculinity.

An attempt to blend together warrior and aristocratic virtues is no easy task. One of the innate difficulties in accomplishing this is that by its very nature a tripartite society assigns differing duties to each class. In Indo-European culture warriors were chosen for valor and rulers for nobility. An attempt to bring these traits together means a blending of class distinction, and this goes against the foundation of the very structure of the society. Men of this period were placed in a position of choosing the class with which they wished to identify—the warrior class or the ruling aristocracy. We will see in the next chapter that this is a dilemma that the middle class will inherit.

Chapter 4

THE BIRTH OF MIDDLE-CLASS MASCULINITY

The "new" contemporary middle-class paradigm of masculinity is a mix of the courtly manners of the aristocracy, the old chivalric ways of knighthood, and the hardiness of the Indo-European warrior. It is important to make note of these differing definitions of masculinity (often distinguished by class differences in contemporary society), which comprise present-day conceptions of masculinity. On the one hand, we have nobility that defines beauty as the extension of virtue. This is juxtaposed with the hardened warriors' notion of valor. With the creation of the middle class, its male members were given both models to emulate, and for each person there ensues a resulting tension over which will be his dominant paradigm.

HISTORICAL ROOTS OF MIDDLE-CLASS MASCULINITY

R. W. Connell (1995) has suggested that there are a number of important historical factors to consider when discussing the roots of the hegemonic concepts of masculinity. (It should be noted that a strong emphasis of Connell's is upon understanding the construction of patriarchy in the Western world, while my emphasis is more upon understanding the paradigmatic evolution of societal conceptions of masculinity. The distinction is that in this work patriarchy is one aspect of the evolving paradigm of masculinity, not its sole focus.) These historical factors are played out on the cultural level amidst a backdrop of the emergence of capitalism in the

North Atlantic. This occurred during the "long sixteenth" century (from about 1450 to 1650), as it was called by French historian Fernard Braudel (cited in Connell, 1995, p. 186). The advent of the Renaissance and the Protestant Reformation marked the beginning of the decrease in the power of the Catholic Church as well as a greater emphasis upon individualism. These two concepts are interrelated as the individual, now considered to be an autonomous soul by the Protestant reformers, had unmediated access (free from the need for priestly intercession) to the Christian God. It should be noted that, as argued here earlier, individualism was a long-held Indo-European value. However, this individualism was permitted to manifest itself only within prescribed cultural limits. The violation of these cultural standards led to an outcast status within the shame-based Indo-European culture. We will see later that as the Church's influence gave way even further in the twentieth century, the scientific/medical field willingly took its place, setting the cultural parameters for acceptable masculinity (see chapter 6, "Psychology's Myth of Masculinity").

Connell (1995) has further suggested that growing imperialism among the Atlantic states (including Spain, Portugal, Great Britain, and the Netherlands) and the United States, Russia, and Italy led to the spreading of the ethic of hegemonic masculinity. This, along with growing urban development in such cities as London and Antwerp, led to a fundamentally different way of life, which included an emphasis upon the Protestant work ethic. A man now was measured by his commitment to work and subsequent accomplishments that came from it, such as gaining property and wealth. One needs to be careful when considering Connell's observation because he was speaking of an emerging middle-class definition of masculinity, not that of the aristocracy. We do not expect the nobility to pound the hammer or push the plow as the middle class should. However, Connell has suggested that it was the gentry (or heritage-based landowners) who were important in setting standards, which include appropriate masculinity within the culture. The gentry were closely aligned with the state, filling such positions as administrators or military officers. They continued to be ruled by the code of honor and used violence when necessary. To this end, they bore arms and found satisfaction in the duel.

Finally, Connell (1995) has suggested that revolution and civil war helped turn the social order upside down. These events had a major impact on the shaping of the definition of middle-class masculinity. It is important to consider social class and/or class distinction in this process, as the gentry and the middle class seemingly coexisted, with the former occupying a higher place in the socioeconomic status. The gentry were more aligned with the descendants of the old aristocracy, whereas the middle class aspired to move up from their present status. Perhaps we can consider the gentry as the upper middle class in the new social order, helping bridge the notions borrowed from the old aristocracy for the emerging middle class.

Also placing emphasis upon social class, historian George Mosse (1996) began his study of the birth of the modern stereotype of masculinity in Western culture in the eighteenth century. He has argued that Europe's dominant aristocracy grudgingly yielded to the rise of a middle class. This new middle class, made up of professional, bureaucratic, and commercial peoples, found themselves in a bewildering position and thus turned to old chivalrous ideals as a paradigm to guide them. In many ways it makes sense that they would recycle an old cultural paradigm, turning to the ruling class (even if from days gone by) for a guide by which to pattern their behavior.

Further solidifying this new paradigm for the middle class was the advent of standing armies and universal conscription. The soldier became one of the potential ideals for the middle-class man. His ideal character-istics included being physically tough, not complaining in the midst of difficulty, carrying a quiet strength, and constraining emotions. Mosse (1996) has argued that the setting of the Napoleonic Wars lead to the culmination of the solider as the stereotype of masculinity. Being in the army allowed for the indoctrination of this new middle class as its mem-bers were taught to be good soldiers.

The solider not only became a potential template for the middle-class hegemonic masculine ideal but also provided a window of opportunity for social advancement. As the need for standing armies grew in this period, there arose an opportunity for members of the nonaristocracy to take a more active role in performing the military functions formerly carried out only by nobility/knights. A middle-class solider could become an officer. This was a position that traditionally had been the military legacy of the knight aristocracy.

Mark Girouard (1981) has further argued that prior to the late nineteenth century the notion of being an English gentleman was exclusive to the ruling class. He also maintains that the ruling class attempted to fight off mounting criticisms and keep some level of power and influence by yield-ing to the middle class an opportunity for social advancement. Middle-class men were given the opportunity to become "gentlemen," the defining mark of upper social class. For the middle class, this presented not only an opportunity to claim a piece of the power that had formerly been held by the ruling class, it was also a chance to gain respectability. In the pre-middle-class era a gentleman was made from two things: pedigree and honorable actions. (Later, education also became a mark of the gentleman.) We see a similar emphasis upon pedigree and honorable actions reflected as far back as early PIE culture. The middle-class gentleman could now bypass pedigree with education. However, he was still considered second best to the man who was born into his social position. There also grew an increasing emphasis upon viewing anyone who acted as a gentleman, regardless of class, as being a gentleman. This notion added a semipermeability to social class (at least in theory) for the middle class.

As more of the reins of power slowly moved into the hands of the middle class, their task was to establish a nonaristocracy that could guide the state of political affairs (Mosse, 1996). The upward movement of the middle class was accomplished in part through male socialization paradigms that included education and proper training. Organizations, such as the Boy Scouts and the Young Men's Christian Association (YMCA), and institutions, such as public schools, brought chivalrous ideas to the middle class. They gave boys specific instructions on how to conduct themselves properly. For instance, in the Boy Scouts there was an emphasis upon cleanliness, courtesy, and being prepared. By the 1830s the education system in England was reformed to reflect two major foci—the chapel, where a boy was supposed to learn proper morality, and the schoolyard, where he supposed to gain mastery over his body and learn fair play. A boy became a gentleman and built proper character in part through the old Indo-European ways of physical challenge, now encompassed within contemporary sport. Team sports, such as cricket and rugby, were transformed into imaginary chivalric battlefields. According to Jonathan Gathorne-Hardy, "A truly chivalrous football player . . . was never guilty of lying, or deceit, or meanness, whether of word or action" (1978, p. 147).

Stained glass, statues, and trophies with chivalrous and knightly themes began to appear in the schools. Models of masculinity included the Arthurian and the heroes of Greek myth, such as Perseus and Theseus (Kingsley, 1856), who rescued ladies in distress. In this retelling of Arthurian tales, a strong emphasis was placed upon shaping young men to assume Victorian morality. For instance, Tennyson's Arthur uttering the words to Guinevere "For I was ever virgin save for thee" ("Guinevere," 1.554) echoes the Victorian-era value of purity. In this case purity connotes having sexual relations only with someone you love, not virginity. When adding the morality aspect to the recycling of the old warrior ethic, the paradigm evolved into "muscular Christianity." This is basically a recycling of the warrior-aristocracy class's notion of chivalry, with that Middle Ages' notion now becoming a guiding template for the middle class.

Middle-class men could now gain access to the two competing models of an ideal man—the gentleman and the warrior. Just as this seemed to generate competing masculine templates during the Middle Ages, so it left middle-class men in a similar quandary in the eighteenth–twentieth centuries. Could the middle-class man have both valor and nobility? Or must he settle for one at the expense of the other?

On the European continent, we see another important development that helped create the hegemonic masculine template for the middle class. A great importance was placed on gymnastics as a tool for training in the manliness ethic (Mosse, 1996). J. C. F. Guts Muth, in "Gymnastics for Youth" (1804/1880), and later writer Fredrich Ludwig Jahn, in "German Gymnastics" (1816), both viewed modern manliness as a continuation of the chivalric ideal of speaking the truth and protecting the weak. Guts Muth argued for the importance of physical training for the youth and the military of Germany. He saw beauty in the physical prowess of athletes, comparing them to Apollo. He found the climate in public schools caused by the reformation after the Napoleonic Wars open to his idea of incorporating gymnastics into the curriculum. Jahn took this notion further and added a patriotic aspect to gymnastics training. He argued that gymnastic exercise was "the lifeline of the German people" (p. 489), stressing the importance of physical training not only within the military. He viewed military exercises as essential for the character development of the nation's youth, and he developed war games in which one group would try to capture another. These games were meant to develop both physical well-being and a manly character. Again we see the attempted fusion of the military ethic and middle-class manhood. The gymnast, Jahn argued, must be "chaste, fearless, truthful and ready to bear arms" (p. 233). He stressed the importance of group activities, though individual accomplishments were recognized too. The attire for youth was changed to identical outfits that showed body contours (no protruding stomachs were allowed). The "militarization of masculinity" was well under way (Mosse, p. 44).

From the French Revolution onward, masculinity, gymnastics, and military ideals were intertwined. Mosse (1996) has suggested that the duel was a sign that this new masculinity was becoming a part of the middle class. While the weapons and the level of intensity varied from country to country, the duel allowed the middle class to find satisfaction in a way that had only previously been available to the knights of the aristocracy. The duel, however, still retained a snobbish twist in Germany, where it was believed that only about 5 percent of the population was honorable enough to seek satisfaction via dueling. In opposition to this, in France all men could duel as a sign of their civic manhood.

MASCULINE BEAUTY AND SOCIAL CLASS

While clearly the bellicose nature of the warrior is one of the driving forces behind what we know as middle-class masculinity in the Western world, another aspect of masculinity must be considered when examining the dynamic tensions men face in Western culture—masculine beauty. Again, this appears to be a concept that stems from the aristocracy's definition of masculinity, and it is both more accepted and elaborated on from their perspective. We saw this earlier in medieval courtly ornamentation. Medieval critics accused some men, those who wore tight tunics, curled their hair, and used effeminate gestures, of going too far with the process of beautification. This type of personal carriage was seen by some as a sexual enticement to both women and men—an unacceptable standard for the warrior class's definition of masculinity of the time, but perhaps less offensive to the ruling aristocracy. Those who adhered to the warrior code pejoratively dismissed these beautiful men as sodomites and the antithesis of true manliness.

And yet the Middle Ages' notion of masculine beauty seems to be a recycling of an idea that has its origin in ancient Greek culture, wherein physical beauty was seen as a reflection of inner harmony. For the ancient Greeks, powerful men (both those of valor and nobility) conveyed a presence of beauty resulting from their masculine virtue and strength. This concept of natural beauty is distinct from the medieval artificial enhancement of physical appearance previously discussed. We see in the heroic stories of valor such as Cuchuliann's and Lancelot's that they were regarded as demigods for their warrior prowess, and this process was reflected by or extended into their physical carriage and appearance. In these cases both women and men are drawn to their presence, and this attraction is seen as an extension of their masculine virtue.

Mosse (1996) has argued that masculine beauty is an integral component in the making of modern middle-class masculinity. He traces this idea back to the influence of Johann Joachim Winckelmann (1717–1768), an archaeologist and art historian, who was celebrated in many German universities as a "giver of light" in regard to civilization. From his youth forward, Winckelmann was obsessed with rediscovering the beauty of Greek sculpture, the only medium in his opinion able to convey the multidimensionality of truth. Winckelmann typically analyzed statues of young athletes whose bodies conveyed harmony, power, virility, and self-control—best summed up as "noble simplicity and quiet grandeur" (cited in Mosse, 1996, p. 29). Examples of such sculptures included *Apollo of Belvedere* and *Laocoön and His Sons Strangled by Snakes*. With regard to the first work of art, Goethe wrote in 1771, "Apollo of Belvedere, why do you show yourself to us in all of your nakedness, making us ashamed of our own?" (Hering, 1931, p. 47). Winckelmann describes the pain that Laocoön's body feels, but, due to the greatness of his soul he is able to achieve inner harmony and remains tranquil in the midst of the storm. While other observers of this statue may see the pain in the face of the subject, it is the paradigm of quiet, strong masculinity it conveys that is most important for Winckelmann. Winckelmann's own same-sex desire is not irrelevant in this matter, as he came to view supreme beauty in the male rather than female form. For him, the male form is never androgynous; rather, masculine beauty is devoid of the feminine.

Later, in the early part of the twentieth century, the issue of masculine beauty was carried forward as the middle class continued to wrestle with this cultural dynamic. Kevin White (1993) has suggested that sex appeal, a gentle, nonthreatening eroticism, came further into vogue for men in the early twentieth century. This ideal of masculine beauty found expression in terms of a male who placed greater emphasis upon physical appeal, including having white teeth, perfectly combed hair, and a slim waistline. Are these definitions so different from the ornamented gentlemen of previous historical periods? It is curious to examine fashion advertisements that were directed toward upper-class men of the day. Some clearly seem to emphasize the nobility aspects of masculinity (being well tailored, using a walking stick) and others are directed more toward rugged individualism (e.g., consider a pair of riding boots advertised with more than its share of western flair).

Tom Pendergast (2000) uses the examination of men's magazines as a tool to understand at the microlevel this new cultural paradigm of masculinity. They may also be included as powerful influences on male socialization. Pendergast suggests that until the 1920s the Victorian notion of masculinity was prominently displayed in magazines, with articles emphasizing the personality and character needed to succeed. Thereafter, magazines such as *Esquire* also took up the descriptive and prescriptive functions of manhood by underscoring the importance not only of work but also of leisure, how one dressed, and what one ate and drank—in short, of lifestyle. While Pendergast does suggest that magazine editors played a prominent role in trying to sell this new image and with it generate more revenues through the sale of their periodicals, he still places a strong emphasis on the middle class itself contributing to its own emerging definition.

In the making of modern middle-class masculinity, it is important to consider the powerful influence of the changing economy of the nineteenth century upon concepts of male beauty. With the influence of the Industrial Revolution, the turn-of-the-century U.S. economy had shifted from a small-shop-based capitalism to one based largely upon large-scale corporations (Pendergast, 2000). This change occurred in the context of other new social forces, such as an influx of immigrants, increases in population density within urban areas, and a new availability of leisure time and activities. There developed within the middle class an emphasis on the consumption of goods. This had a powerful impact upon male gender norms. The latter half of the nineteenth century was marked by the prominence of Victorian masculinity based upon property ownership, which assured economic success; practicing self-control; and developing character. In *Meaning of Manhood: Constructions of Masculinity in Victorian America*, Mark C. Carnes and Clyde Griffen (1990) suggest that this was the prominent paradigm of the time (though they also suggest that this was one choice among a variety of competing paradigms during this period).

As middle-class men sought leisure and recreation in this new period of consumerism, they found new venues for courtship. There was also a new emphasis upon women's bodies as commodities that men could purchase as in the process of courting (Highwater, 1991). Men might also use their own physical charm as a method to allure women. Kevin White's *First Sexual Revolution* (1993) highlights the notion that the masculine ideal that emerged, replacing the Victorian paradigm, was one that valued appearance, personality, and sexuality.

CONCLUSION

Throughout our examination of Western culture there have been differing masculinities within different social classes. This has particular import for understanding the making of modern middle-class masculinity. As highlighted in previous chapters, the ruling aristocracy and the warrior class had differing and competing models of masculinity. These stemmed from the differing functions that each played in society. The warrior was chosen for valor, whereas the ruler was chosen for nobility. The paradigm of the ruling aristocracy of the Indo-Europeans suggests a code of masculinity in which aristocrats kept a safe distance from the warrior ethic. Too much valor within the nobility may lead to an unfavorable, zane status. Likewise, a warrior with too much courtly refinement would be viewed with suspicion by his contemporaries. Cultural conflict arose when medieval chivalry was created and attempted to blend together aspects of these differing definitions of prototypical masculinity. The middle class inherited this cultural dilemma that emphasized differences in the masculine ideal. This paradigmatic conflict was not well resolved by either the ruling aristocracy or the warrior class before the advent of the middle class.

The middle class attempted to deal with this dilemma by subdividing its own caste even further into upper-middle and middle/working classes. The warrior ethic seems to have eventually resonated with the middle/working class, as seen in the cultural icons of the American cowboy, the frontiersman, and the rugged individualist of the nineteenth–twentieth centuries. The masculinity of the ruling/upper class was more aligned with the essence of the gentleman and the country gentry. In essence, the middle-class solution to the two competing masculinities is the same one the mythmakers of the Middle Ages attempted. Masculinity is dichotomized as reflecting either refinement or valor. These, in turn, are attached to social standing whereby refinement is indicative of a higher standing and valor alone may be suspect of a lower standing. It is only the rare individual in myth or reality who can straddle both worlds successfully. The noble knight of chivalric fame seems to represent an ongoing attempt to synthesize these two competing models of masculinity. In Arthurian myth, the knight embodies the valor of the old warrior ethic but also protects the weak and helpless, while always showing the refinement of the courtly way. Perhaps that is why the noble knight is an enduring symbol that found expression throughout the nineteenth and twentieth centuries as a model toward which men should strive. The men of the new, burgeoning middle class found themselves struggling with issues of nobility and valor. The middle-class man was now attempting to be a gentleman through action, not pedigree.

As the middle class arose, it looked to the two earlier paradigms (i.e., warrior and aristocrat) that highlighted how men should ideally be. With the inherent conflicts in this paradigm of two masculinities, why did the middle class chose to pick up where men of the Middle Ages left off? It is difficult to discern if the use of these former paradigms was due to a nostalgic romanticizing of the past or was for more practical notions that these known models gave as form and guidance to the new middle class. In all likelihood, it was some combination of these sociocultural forces.

Chapter 5

THE COWBOY MYTH

The medieval model of the elite aristocracy and the warrior caste were transformed eventually into one of the models for normative middle-class Western masculinity. The warrior component is further elaborated on here as we examine one of the most enduring middle-class symbols of American masculinity—the cowboy. Though the time of the cowboy was a relatively brief period at the end of the nineteenth and beginning of the twentieth centuries, the cowboy myth lives on, occupying a prominent role in the American cultural myth of masculinity. It represents the next evolution in the template of American middle-class masculinity, following the rugged individualist, the frontiersman, and the mountain man. While seeming to be a relatively new contribution to the evolution of masculinity, its roots are nonetheless based in the Indo-European past. Aspects of the European warrior ethic found their way into southern U.S. culture, and the resulting cowboy mythology firmly rooted itself within the American paradigm of middle-class masculinity.

While the reign of the cowboy was relatively brief—some twenty-five years in its prime—it left a lasting legacy (Frantz & Choate, 1955). One may wonder if the cowboy actually is a composite template of images of American masculinity that came before it. These would include mountain man and frontiersman images, such as those of Daniel Boone and Lewis and Clark exploring the unknown wilderness. They would also include the Indian fighter and the rancher, functioning as a part of the wildness they tried to tame. Some scholars have argued that the American cowboy had his first appearance in the American Revolution, as a Tory known for carrying arms and plundering cattle (Frantz & Choate, 1955). Slotkin (1985) has argued for a hero personification that evolved as U.S. society moved westward. Tom Sawyer got his sense of hero from James Fenimore Cooper and Horatio Alger, from Ned Buntline, just as later generations got theirs from Owen Wister's Virginian (1902/1968) and, still later, from the John Wayne persona. The myth of the cowboy way of life came to symbolize a simple, tough, and chivalrous approach. The cultural myth typically portrayed the cowboy as a white male no older than his mid-thirties, lacking formal education but schooled in the areas of honor, firearms, physical toughness, and a strong sense of individualism. Frantz and Choate have argued the following:

> Ideally the American cowboy was a superb horseman, which as a fact he was; an expert of the fast draw and the use of a Colt revolver, which he might have been; a dead shot with a Winchester; brave beyond question; always on the side of justice, even if that justice was a bit stern at times; the defender of virtuous women; the implacable foe of the Indian; and a man to whom honor and integrity came naturally. (p. 72)

The cowboy hero is soft-spoken and modest but capable of extreme violence, which he uses to right wrongs that are both personal and communal (Erisman, 1997). Weston (1985) has suggested that later versions of the cowboy myth follow standard plots that include exposing wrongdoers who try to hurt the town, the territory, and/or individual families. These wrongdoers can include saloon owners, empire builders, bullies, outlaw gangs, carpetbaggers, and the murderers of family members, including the hero's father. It is no strain to see the influence of the Indo-European warrior (discussed in chapter 2) and also that of the chivalric code. In this definition of the cowboy, a mounted warrior who stands for good protects women and children and is loyal and brave to a fault. He achieves the fame that does not decay while serving and protecting the community. This credo would come to epitomize one paradigm of real masculinity within the middle class. After the Civil War, cowboys came to be viewed as semi-Southern cavaliers for whom a Southern cavalry hat served as a sombrero. Many young men went west to find fortune and adventure after the war. Even amidst the satire of the day, such as Mark Twain's *Connecticut Yankee in King Arthur's Court*, the South maintained its loyalty to chivalric ways. In any event, the cowboy represented the next transformation of the Indo-European warrior/knight: "The knight and cowboy are nothing but the same Saxon of different environments" (Wister, 1895, p. 608). And, there is

> something romantic about him. He lives on horseback . . . he fights on horseback as did the knights of chivalry; he goes armed with a strange new weapon which he uses ambidextrously and precisely; he swears like a trooper, drinks like a fish, wears clothes like an actor, and fights like a devil. He is gracious to ladies, reserved toward strangers, generous toward friends, and brutal toward enemies. He is a cowboy, a typical Westerner. (Walter Prescott Webb, 1931, p. 496)

Indeed, this is the stuff of dime novels in the later part of the nineteenth century and the early twentieth century. Fiction writers such as Zane Gray and entertainers who appeared in Wild Bill Hitchcock's *Wild West Show* created and confirmed this cultural myth. Other important works also contributed to the twentieth-century version of this cultural template. The western classics *The Virginian* (Wister, 1902/1988) and *Lonesome Dove* (McMurtry, 1986) both confirmed this cowboy mythology. In the former book, the Virginian goes through the cowboy cycle of defeating the bad guys through his toughness while demonstrating both a sense of honor and courage and the ability to use physical violence in a justified manner.

There are also many chivalric themes in *Lonesome Dove*, the story of two Texas Rangers who gained notoriety for the courage they demonstrated while trying to civilize the Texas frontier. They fought bandits, fierce Indians, and the like. The story takes place in the later years of their lives, when Captain Call and Captain McCrae have taken their surviving troops and formed the Hatcreek Gang, a livery stable in south Texas. Deciding that they will be the first ranchers to raise cattle in Montana, they set out with their herd. During the course of this drive, they perform the chivalric act of rescuing a woman from the hands of antichivalrous outlaws. This deed occurs in the old style of heroes. McCrae single-handedly rides in and does battle with seven outlaws. Later in the story Call goes into what could be described as a frenzied rage as he nearly beats a man to death for what he describes as rude behavior. It is only through intervention by his friend McCrae that Call refrains from beating the man to death. McCrae ropes his friend and is prepared to knock him unconscious with the butt of his pistol. Call, in the midst of his rage, does not recognize those around him and will attack anyone who tries to stop him. This is reminiscent of the Indo-European warriors, including the Vikings and the Irish hero Cuchuliann. Returning from battle, Cuchuliann is still in a battle rage and does not recognize his family or friends, placing both in jeopardy. Cuchuliann ends his battle fury only after women expose their breasts to distract him long enough for the men of his tribe to seize him and dunk him in vats of water to diminish the fever of battle.

The cowboy also demonstrates the firmness of the code of the warrior/ chivalric knight. In *The Virginian*, the protagonist hangs his former best friend, Steve, for joining an outlaw gang. Similarly, in *Lonesome Dove* Call and McCrae catch and hang a former ranger friend who has fallen in with a group of bad men. They hang him with the respect and care of friends, but there is no talk of letting him go. Instead, they cite the code of the west, which cannot be broken even for former rangers.

Adding to the cowboy persona was the myth of the Great American Desert (Frantz & Choate, 1955). In 1541, the Spanish explorer Coronado wrote his king that the western region of North America was a vast desert. Later explorers did much toward extending this old story, categorizing it as a fearsome place uninhabitable by man. Part of the cowboy mythology was that this breed of rugged individualist who rode mustangs, carried six-guns, and could herd longhorns with horns three to five feet wide not only survived this inhospitable frontier but drew strength from it and its wild, untamed nature. We see in later post-Western plots and stories— such as in Paul Newman's portrayal of Hud—the bitter cowboy of the 1950s separated from his true source of strength by cars, technology, and modernity in general (Weston, 1985).

Artist Fredric Remington also reflected the code of masculinity in his nineteenth- and early-twentieth-century works of art. Remington was taken with the myth of the Wild West and its tales of cowboys and Indians. He recognized that the west was vanishing, and he wished to capture its essence in his paintings and sculpture. In Remington's paintings, the cowboy is pictured with his horse in many harrowing situations, such as being chased by Indians or in the middle of a shootout. What initially seems peculiar about the subjects in Remington's art is that the animals are usually the ones who carry the emotion in the scene. That is, in the midst of life-threatening situations the cowboy exhibits a calm tranquility. Remington is, thus, using the animals' display of fear or anguish to inform the observer that something special is occurring. Despite the danger, the cowboy is in charge of the situation and his emotions. In one of Remington's nineteenth-century oil paintings, entitled *Aid to a Comrade*, three cowboys are riding abreast with charging Indians in the background. The comrade in the middle has fallen from his horse and is about to strike the ground full force and be trampled. This work, which was originally titled *Beyond First Aid*, shows the tranquility and calmness not only of the two mounted cowboys but also of the one who is about to perish. It is by looking to the emotion of the horses, wild-eyed and fearful, that we capture the essence of the strength of this new breed of man. This is a reflection of the archaeologist and art historian Winckelmann's observation of the quiet masculine strength in the midst of turmoil seen in Greek art (as mentioned in chapter 4). These works of art, be they Remington's paintings or Greek statuary, are markers of the template of masculinity of their time period. They perform a prescriptive function to the observer by stating what masculinity should be.

RADIO AND TELEVISION COWBOYS

With the advent of radio, television, and the movies, a new mode of mythmaking and socialization was created. Where once there was the fire circle of the local tribe, now there was the family television room; where once legend and myth were presented for entertainment and socialization in the Nordic/Germanic great hall, now there were movies. In this new brand of cultural indoctrination, television series of the 1950s and 1960s such as *Rawhide, The Virginian, The Rifleman, Gunsmoke, Bonanza, Big Valley, The Wild Wild West, Have Gun Will Travel,* and countless others were born. The theme song of *Have Gun Will Travel* clearly points to the influence of chivalric notion in its conception. Dapper, black-clad Paladin is a high-priced gun for hire. His strong sense of ethics soon establishes that he is a man of morals and conscience trying to settle disputes without violence. Paladin is portrayed as an educated West Point–trained officer who served in the Civil War. He is also a dandy with a taste for fine food and clothing. His calling card features a picture of a paladin—the white knight in chess—and the inscription Have Gun Will Travel. This portrayal, of course, paralleled the historic and ongoing adventures of both the courtly gentleman and the chivalrous knight-errant. Paladin, whose very name connects us directly to these earlier themes, is a righteous gun for hire. His adventures are about righting the wrongs of the innocent and the oppressed. The term *knight* is even used in the show's theme song.

CONCLUSION

The sociocultural forces arising from the move into an untamed land called for the creation of a masculine paradigm that could tame the Wild West. There is reason to believe that as Americans moved into the untamed west, the masculine icons of the frontiersman and the mountain man were precursors for the cowboy. These symbols spoke to bravery, honor, and, sometimes, foolhardiness—themes consistent with the PIE masculine templates. The cowboy icon built upon these early templates by bringing chivalric aspects of the knight to the western frontier. The cowboy was a mounted, sombrero-wearing knight errant looking for adventure, righting the wrongs of evildoers, and making a name for himself as he saved the community. He was highly capable of using violence in the extreme, in true Indo-European fashion, to accomplish his goals. We like to think of him as using this power only when confronting evildoers who—much like the three-headed monster the Indo-European hero Trito defeats—deserve this type of treatment. The cowboy uses righteous indignation to fuel his fury when setting things right.

A tangible expression of the making of the cowboy into a middle-class icon can be seen in various dime novels, other books, and movies of the twentieth century. While the historic precedent of Indo-European culture allowed only the warriors and aristocrats to carry arms, now a little boy with a cowboy hat and imaginary horse could carry a toy gun too. This infusion of chivalric values into middle-class America furthered warrior values as an acceptable icon of masculinity. This evolutionary icon of masculinity was concerned with expanding the boundaries of his territory for familial/communal reasons and for his own desire to achieve the fame that does not decay by leaving a permanent mark. The second caste of the Indo-European culture—the warrior—had become the ideal for which many middle-class men strove.

Chapter 6

PSYCHOLOGY'S MYTH
OF MASCULINITY

At the beginning of the twentieth century, important aspects of the knightly code that originated in the Indo-European warrior/aristocracy castes fused with Judeo-Christian tradition and lived on. The middle class, searching for guidance as well as an opportunity for social mobility, borrowed heavily from the chivalric tradition. Elements from this paradigm were incorporated into the budding middle class's guiding ethos for normative masculinity. However, some cultural tension remained, centering on issues of what seems to be a forced choice of striving for either valor or nobility. We will see that class distinctions make a successful incorporation of both roles into an individual's personal definition of masculinity nearly impossible. Also left unresolved is the contemporary questioning of the Victorian masculinity, including the preeminence of the values of character, hard work, and self-control. These standards are challenged by a consumer masculinity wherein personality, sex appeal, and leisure define values.

In more recent times, attempts to understand and define masculinity took yet another direction with the development of the disciplines of sexology and psychoanalysis. As the nineteenth century drew to a close, both sexology and psychoanalysis were beginning to take root in the Western mind. Both have contributed much to contemporary notions of masculinity. In this chapter, we will discuss how each has left a lasting impact on how we conceptualize the development of masculine identity. We will also see how the overriding scientific paradigm that dominated the early part of the twentieth century—notably the mechanistic model of Descartes—contributed to solidifying the notion of the body as a machine and helped guide proper and improper ways for this machine to develop and operate. The developmental theories that arise from sexology and psychoanalytic thought are the foundations for the contemporary Western blueprint of becoming a man. These notions are more formally voiced in some gender-role theories that gave both descriptions of what men should be and blueprints for achieving that identity or status. This chapter concludes with an examination of a number of competing gender-role paradigms in the twenty-first century.

Psychology and its notions about gender roles for men are also a form of myth. That is, while the new social science attempts to provide a more credible platform on which to stand when discussing so-called objective notions of gender, these viewpoints are still in large part a socially constructed entity. The science of psychology and gender roles is constructed in a social context that reflects current attitudes regarding gender ideals for men and appropriate methods of socialization. This is in keeping with the other myths we have examined thus far. To that end, psychology and the gender-role paradigms that follow are—at least in part—still mythic in form. They perform the same function as cherished myths from days gone by in giving direction and tangible ideals toward which men should strive. It is this infusion of scientific inquiry with objective truth that leads to the growing power of psychology in the nineteenth–twentieth centuries. Zealots may maintain, "But these are scientific findings, and therefore they must be true." What we may fail to appreciate is that while scientific inquiry may point us toward seeing objective truth, it may not always allow us to examine it clearly in the moment. As I will demonstrate in this chapter, cherished theories in the social sciences in regard to gender issues come into and out of credibility over time. Thus what appears to be an examination of philosophy and social science here may seem to some a radical departure from the mythic exploration of the previous chapters. However, these aspects are merely a more sophisticated version of myth than those we have previously discussed. We will see the incorporation of mythic icons and stories of old into these newer versions of myth. We will also see how modern paradigms of male socialization and behavior are provided by science/psychology. These paradigms of thought sometimes use icons that act as the personification of their models. That is, they provide specific heroes and zanes within their paradigms. These act as explicit and implicit guidelines for men. A prime example of the zane icon in nineteenth- and twentieth-century psychology is so-called psychologically regressed men. These are men who have failed to incorporate the hegemonic notion of masculinity. Others dominate them, they lack masculine prowess, and they may even have same-sex desire.

What is different in this chapter is its telling of the tale of masculinity in more scientific terms. In places, it may read less like the telling of a myth and more like an excerpt from a journal article. This may be due to my shortcomings as a storyteller as I try to speak objectively about paradigms and myths that are very much a part of my personal legacy. Perhaps this chapter would have less of a scientific feel and more of a mythic one if were written some time in the future when these paradigms of masculinity seem less like objective truth and more like the myths they are.

What can be drawn from the need for scientific language in this discussion is our cultural emphasis upon science in our understanding of masculinity. Culturally, we are under the impression that science has finally led us to a place where we can discover the truth about men. We trust that science will show us the way and provide us with the answers. What we fail to grasp is that much of this new, purportedly enlightened thinking asks many of the same questions that have been asked for millennia. What do men need to do to be valued by society? How do we go about instilling these values into boys so they can grow up to be proper men? The answers provided by these paradigms of science (i.e., those of sexology, psychoanalysis, and so forth) differ from those offered by the earlier paradigms discussed here in terms of both content and their use of more awe-inspiring jargon, but ultimately they too are threads of the socially constructed mythic world of gender roles.

BODY AS MACHINE

René Descartes, the mechanistic French philosopher of the seventeenth century, set the tone for science for centuries to come. This has particular import for its influence on the mythology of gender roles and the body. Highwater (1991) has highlighted the importance of Descartes's mechanistic beliefs as they applied to the cultural understanding of the human body. Just as the universe was reduced to mechanistic aspects (a clock wound by the hands of God), so too was the human body viewed as being a subsystem of the greater universal machine, which could be deciphered in similar fashion. Descartes likened the body to an automaton, a mechanized creature much like the fountains of his day that were made in animal form and propelled to animation by water that ran through them. And, just as the automaton and the clock had internal workings that propelled them to life, so did the corporeal aspects of the circulatory system drive the body of man. This mechanistic perspective suggested that all living things were automatons, subject to proper and improper care and management.

Descartes's influence was felt in the nineteenth-century science of sexual taxonomy known as sexology. Sexology began as a study of sexual normality and thus needed a foil to help define what was abnormal. It is commonly held that as the church began to wane as an influence for checking undesirable behaviors in the populous, the void was filled by medical science. It is here that Descartes's mechanistic view of the world had its greatest influence. The body was not to be abused by inappropriate sexual acts and perversions, any more than one would overwind a clock or use the wrong fluids in a machine. A man's body, too, was subject to the strain of overuse and misuse. Further, bodily fluids were a limited commodity and not to be wasted on unnecessary sexual discharge such as masturbation. This activity could leave the body weakened, rendering a man unprepared to grapple with life's challenges. This is the root of the commonly held sports mythology of abstinence while in training. Engaging in sexual activity of any kind would cause a man to lose his competitive edge. Similarly, the belief that diet could help control the body's urges so as to keep fighting men strong is the motivation behind giving saltpeter to military troops. A frontier example of this theme is the song "The Yellow Rose of Texas," which is actually a tribute to the Mexican prostitute (the Yellow Rose) who slept with the Mexican general Antonio López de Santa Anna and thus weakened him the night before the Battle of San Jacinto, in which Texas won its independence.

The same guiding principle for adult men was also applied to boys, who must avoid unnecessary sexual expenditure. To this end, men such as Will Keith Kellogg and Sylvester Graham invented breakfast and snack foods (respectively) that would act as antimasturbation aids. The belief was that keeping boys busy and filled with food would curb their sexual appetite. Within this paradigm, young men also needed further guidance to help them grow up correctly. With sexology categorizing stereotypical effeminate men and, especially, the new category of homosexuals as those whose development went awry, we are given the ultimate zane, or gender-identity foil, against which to set normal development. (It has been argued by gender historian Michel Foucault [1980] that homosexuality was a category that did not exist before the nineteenth century.) It is within this paradigm that sexology and, then, Sigmund Freud and other later psycho-analytic writers, would help conceive a normal developmental path in part by telling us what was pathological.

SEXOLOGY AND THE SEXUAL INVERT

Perhaps the most central and enduring aspect of the study of sexology is that of sexual inversion (Prosser, 1998). There has been an overwhelming tendency by historians of sexology to label the sexual invert as homosexual. George Chauncey (1982) has noted that sexual inversion is not the same conceptually as homosexuality. Rather, it refers to a broad range of so-called deviant gender behavior. However, it is often same-sex desire that comes to the forefront in sexology. In fact, sexology enjoyed its most prominent notoriety during the heyday of Havelock Ellis's (1936) writing on the topic of the sexual invert, after which its popularity began to wane. Because of sexology's earlier grappling with same-sex attraction, there was a renewed interest in the discipline in the 1960s and 1970s with the advent of gay studies. Sexual inversion has it roots in nineteenth-century theorists such as Richard von Krafft-Ebing and Ellis.

Richard von Krafft-Ebing

One of the key figures in the development of sexology is Richard von Krafft-Ebing, whose work *Psychopathia Sexualis* was published in twelve editions from 1886 to 1903. Part of his work focuses on the notion of bisexuality, which he suggests is physiologically predetermined in the human fetus. It is at this fetal stage in human development when the person begins to develop either normally or so as to take on inverted forms of sexuality after birth. There is physical residue of the initial bisexual state even in normal adults, as Krafft-Ebing points out using the example of male nipples. In addition, the original bisexuality can produce gradations between the "pure type" of man and woman. That is, some men and women experience only opposite-sex desire and are considered the pure type. Then there are others, who may experience some type of mixed desire for same- and opposite-sex partners who represent the varying degrees of sexual inversion. Krafft-Ebing categorized sexual perversion in four degrees of inversion: bisexuality, homosexuality, transgender sexuality, and intersexuality. While same-sex desire was one of four possible perversions, it became the lasting focus of the sexual invert as well as of sexology as a whole. The gradation of normal and sexual inversion later became important in terms of Krafft-Ebing's diagnosis and subsequent treatment of his patients.

Bleys (1996) has pointed out that sexologists between 1860 and 1918 wrestled with the question of whether sexual inversion, and in particular same-sex desire, was a degenerative condition leading one away from heterosexual desire. Perverse sexuality could be seen as something that civilized cultures left behind as they evolved, unless particular socioemotional factors intervened. For instance, for some sexologists, sexual perversions were considered to be a result of the Industrial Revolution, whereby modern stresses caused the culture to regress (Storr, 1998). According to Krafft-Ebing, all humans share the same bisexuality, but it is the mark of a more advanced culture to move beyond it and clearly differentiate between men and women. More so-called primitive peoples, according to Krafft-Ebing, such as Native Americans, were closer to their original bisexuality and therefore more prone to sexual perversion. However, white European culture, though more evolved, could also be weakened by the modern ills of society.

In terms of etiology and prognosis, Krafft-Ebing concluded that there are two classifications for the various sexual inverts: the congenital and the acquired. In the first type, physiology in the form of neuropathic strands affects a person's ability to advance beyond the original bisexuality. These strands were viewed as being responsible for deviant sexual desires, which could include attraction to both men and women. In the case of the acquired type, corrupting social factors led to perverse sexual desire. Here, the individual regresses to a pathological state due to sociocultural conditions.

Krafft-Ebing outlined the metamorphosis of the acquired sexual inversion:

1. The subject has sexual feelings toward his own sex, but the sexual personality and instinct remain basically normal—in other words, the man will continue to take the active role during sex;

2. The subject's personality is transformed, such that he becomes passive and feels like a woman during sex; this stage is known as "eviration" and resembles congenital inversion;

3. The subject is in a state of transition to a full delusion of having changed sex altogether, with not just psychical feelings but also physical sensation now being affected;

4. The subject, at last believing that he has changed sex completely, falls into paranoia. (quoted in Storr, 1998, p. 16)

Krafft-Ebing discussed a case wherein a doctor in stage 3 of transformation begins to feel that lovemaking with his wife is an act of perversion. More specifically, he feels like a woman and views his lovemaking with his wife as an act of lesbianism. That is, the doctor feels as if he no longer takes the active, virile stance of a man and instead has been transformed into taking a more feminine, passive one. In this case example we see that sexual inversion is not only about same-sex desire but also about improper attitude or behavior that deviates from the stereotypical norm of the man's being active and the woman's being passive. Eventually the doctor fell in love with another woman who had gone through her own sexual transformation into masculinity. In this case the gender roles were reversed, and, while perverse in the sexology sense, in this situation one partner is masculine and the other feminine. Thus it may be constituted as an act of heterosexual love in which one partner is active and the other passive.

Krafft-Ebing also discusses four stages of the congenital sexual invert:

1. Psychical hermaphroditism, where subjects are homosexual but traces of heterosexuality remain;
2. Homosexuality, where there is an inclination towards members of the same sex only;
3. Effemination (in men) or virginity (in women), where there is an inverted sexual instinct;
4. Hermaphroditism or pseudo-hermaphroditism, where the subject's physical form begins to correspond to the inverted sexual instinct so that men's bodies become feminized and women's bodies masculinized. (quoted in Storr, 1998, p. 18)

In *Psychopathia Sexualis*, Krafft-Ebing maintains that the essential feature of the congenital type is the desire for the opposite sex "even to the extent of horror" while simultaneously being drawn to the same sex. He provides a case study of a young man who clearly prefers men but regards sexual relations with women as a "coarsely sensual enjoyment" (p. 221). In another case study, a man who prefers men goes weekly to a brothel where he dresses as a woman and has a female prostitute sexually stimulate him.

Ultimately, whether a case of inversion is of the acquired or the congenital type, Krafft-Ebing seems to have believed that physiology has some influence in the form of neuropathic strands. The congenital type was seen as being driven by biological forces, but even with the acquired type of inversion there was suspicion that neuropathy was also involved. In Krafft-Ebing's view any man with a hereditary nervous weakness should avoid masturbation because this activity could erode male virility and lead to same-sex desire or perversion. This seems to imply that the definition of gender identity in men is seemingly corruptible in the face of ill forces. Moreover, it suggests that socioemotional forces may sooner or later reveal the presence of neuropathic inversion strands. Later, Ellis and poet, cultural critic, and coauthor of *Sexual Inversion* John Adington Symonds would challenge Krafft-Ebing's notion of neuropathic strands. Ellis and Symonds (1897) contested Krafft-Ebing's contention that all humans seem to carry the potential for these neuropathic strands, not just the few who actually show sexual perversion. This repudiated his suspicion that everyone—the congenital and the acquired types as well as those who had no expressed same-sex desire—could have these strands lying dormant, waiting for the right activating force.

Havelock Ellis

Havelock Ellis's work in the field of sexology, in particular with the sexual invert, was quite influential. His early work was controversial to the point of inspiring a legal inquiry that led to the banning of his book *Sexual Inversion* (Ellis & Symonds, 1897) on obscenity charges. George Bedborough, the secretary of the Legitimation League, a radical political group lobbying for legal same-sex unions, was arrested and brought to trial when he unknowingly sold a copy of the book to an undercover police officer in London. A year after the trial police raided the warehouse of Ellis's British publisher and seized his other works, including *Evolution of Modesty, The Phenomena of Sexual Periodicity,* and *Auto-Eroticism.* To some people, this material was obscene, in keeping with the climate of the time, which saw the trial and imprisonment of the noted writer Oscar Wilde for having same-sex relations. Further evidence of this antihomosexual attitude is demonstrated by England's 1885 Labouchère Amendment, which made illegal any "act of gross indecency" between men in public or private. This would later be nicknamed the "Blackmailers' Charter" because of its political divisiveness.

Ellis would later recall in his autobiography that the seizure of his book and the subsequent turbulent events that followed had a large impact upon his work as a sexologist and social reformer. After the raid on the warehouse in which his books were stored, Ellis decided to transfer the publication of his next work to a U.S. publishing house. *Studies in the Psychology of Sex,* originally published during the years 1897–1928, was a seven-volume study of the behavior and sexual physiology of the period. The copyright for this collection eventually went to Random House, who in 1936 reissued it in a more affordable version and made it available for the first time to those outside of the sexology professional circle.

By the 1930s Ellis had become a household name and enjoyed a prestigious place in the professional community. One of his most important contributions was his work that focused upon taking the sexual invert out of the realm of the pathological. Instead, he conceptualized sexual inversion as a biological variation similar to variations in eye color, height, and weight. He objected to the notion of neuropathic strands that categorized sexual inversion as a degenerative condition. However, he did compare individuals who experienced sexual inversion to the "congenital idiot, to the instinctive criminal, to the man of genius" (Ellis & Symonds, 1897, p. 23).

From the perspective of the cultural myth of masculinity, the foundations of sexology—be they Krafft-Ebing's or Ellis's—would seemingly lead one to take a rather cautious if not paranoid stance with regard to the rearing of boys into proper men. This perspective proposes that masculinity can be corrupted into perverse manifestations, and, especially from Krafft-Ebing's perspective, all men (and women) carry the potential for this corruption because of deviant neuropathic strands. To deal with these hypothesized dangers, this period saw the creation of rather grotesque devices, such as spiked penile rings for boys to prevent sexual excitement and masturbation. As mentioned previously, Kellogg and Graham, respectively, developed breakfast and snack foods to curb sexual desire. The notion that there is potential for corruptibility is by no means confined to the turn-of-the-century paradigm of masculinity. We see it manifest in contemporary attempts to raise boys properly through avoiding other corrupting forces, which include the stereotypical notion of the feminine. These are powerful keys to understanding the foundation for the cultural myth of masculinity in more contemporary times. They speak to notions that were socially constructed during a specific time period but that are taken to be abject truth.

PSYCHOANALYSIS

In the cultural myth of masculinity, gender identity, which refers to one's basic sense of maleness and femaleness, has played a prominent role in the history of psychoanalytic thought. The term *sexual identity* is sometimes considered synonymous to *gender identity* but is more precisely a later, more refined construct that includes sexual desire. Freud, of course, assumed the leadership in the discussion of these issues of sex and sexuality as psychology evolved. He argued that biology is destiny in matters of gender identity; that is, men should follow their natural course to become healthy men. Many of his thoughts on sexuality were viewed as controversial both within the community at large as well as within his inner psychoanalytic circle. At times his ideas were considered dangerous to the reputation of the budding psychoanalytic thought. In fact, disagreements on this topic among the inner circle led to the parting of ways with Freud by Carl Jung and Alfred Adler, to name two. Other theorists redefined Freudian thought on sexuality, adding to and honing many of his early ideas. It is important to examine both the early Freudian notion of sexuality as well as the ideas of those who refined it in order to understand historical and current views of male sexuality.

Freudian Sexuality

Just as Descartes's body as a machine idea held importance for his taxonomy of corporality, so did Freud's hydraulic model hold import for his conception of emotion and the mind. In Freud's early writings (typically referred to as the period of "id psychology"), the emphasis was upon a topographical model of the psyche. This included the unconscious, the preconscious, and the conscious realms of the mind. Within the unconscious resided all manner of darkness and evil. These were instinctual and a part of our biology. This concept of the mind was an extrapolation from social Darwinism and was derived from the then-prevailing belief that our ancestors were killer apes. If there were to be a civilization, these wanton instincts and desires had to be kept in check. Freud, however, like all scientists of the day, was still under the Cartesian influence that suggested a mechanistic view of these emotions and instincts. He maintained that the unconscious material in the mind pressed for expression and had to be held in check within the unconscious if not dealt with directly. Freud suggested that neurosis was the compromise between being a society of killer apes, on the one hand, and denying these impulses entirely, on the other.

The early cathartic method employed by psychoanalysis also is in keeping with the hydraulic model of the mind. When Freud was experimenting with hypnosis, he would place his patients in a trance then have them talk about the things that were bothering them. These, of course, included topics that previously were never discussed and were held as taboo; this oftentimes led to an emotional outpouring. Freud noted that this cathartic method often led to temporary symptom reduction. The notion of letting your feelings out has, of course, become a part of therapy and pop-cultural lore—"If you don't express your feelings, you will explode."

In some ways Freud's model—in particular, the conscious versus the unconscious aspects of the individual—seemed to fit well with Victorian society. The Victorian era has long held associations of purity, but the uprightness of the era paradigm was juxtaposed with a seedy underbelly that included the existence of brothels (Highwater, 1991). Important above all else for men of the middle and upper classes was character. Toward this end many Victorian men chose virginity until marriage. However, this so-called virginity meant only that they did not engage in sexual relations with their middle-class fiancées. A middle-class man could be a frequent visitor to a brothel of lower-class women and still remain a "virgin." The period writer Alfred, Lord Tennyson reflects this definition of virginity as he has King Arthur tell Guinevere, "For I was ever virgin save for thee" ("Guinevere," 1.554).

From Seduction Theory to Libido

In his early work Freud wrestled with the source of the neurotic behavior he saw in his hysterical, mostly female, upper-class clientele. He first postulated the seduction theory of neurosis, which arose from the many stories he heard from his female patients who reported having had their sexual boundaries violated by a male family member, usually their father, brother, or uncle. In his famous exchange of letters with his colleague Wilhelm Fliess, Freud shared his thought that this was the source of the neurotic conflict (Mason, 1984). Fliess responded that what Freud was implying would cast moral doubt not only on the men of their time but, ultimately, also on psychoanalytic thought. Fliess, among others, urged Freud to rethink his position, which he did. Freud began to explain the reports of these hysterical women as their fantasies of wishing to have sexual relations with a father figure. Others (Krull, 1986; Kupfersmid, 1992, 1995) have argued that the real reason Freud renounced his position on sexual seduction was that he himself was molested as a child by a male close to him; some even believe it was his father. Those who support this conjecture maintain that Freud felt conflicted about being disloyal to his father, whom he loved very much, and felt internal pressure to drop the theory. When Freud presented this new fantasy interpretation to Dora, a client of his who actually had been molested by her father, she abruptly left the consulting room and never came back.

Freud, much to the chagrin of twentieth-century Victorians, suggested that children are born as sexual beings with sexual feelings for their parents. The full meaning of this concept is often misunderstood in practice and in theory. Initially, *libido* did stand for the sexual energy of the individual. Later, however, in his essay entitled "Observations on Wild Analysis," (1910/1963) Freud discussed *liben,* which he described as a mental representation aligned more with the expression of tender feelings than with physical sex. (Oftentimes an evolution of theory is lost when it is incorporated into pop psychology.) This is not to say that fantasized incest was not an important element in Freud's conceptualizations. However, the relational aspect of his theory has often been overshadowed, and his concept of libido has been misinterpreted as involving only a sexual component.

As a part of his stage theory, Freud postulated that the individual must negotiate developmental challenges represented by the movement of libidinal energy through a progression of parts of the body, that is, oral, anal, phallic, and genital. It is during the phallic stage that the masculine development begins to take form as the foundation of masculine development is established. The boy renounces the connection with his mother and instead counteridentifies with his father. This identification takes place within the context of the Oedipal complex.

The Oedipal complex is based upon the Greek tragedy of Oedipus, the king of Thebes who unwittingly slew his father and married his mother. Later he goes mad, blinding himself when he discovers the truth. The Oedipal complex suggests there is a longing for the opposite-sex parent and, in the boy's case, a fear that his bigger, more powerful rival and father will destroy or castrate him for having such unbounded thoughts and desires. The complex is resolved when the boy realizes that he will never be able to wrest his mother away from his more powerful father and begins instead to make peace with his father. In doing so, the boy begins to internalize and emulate his father's gender-role behavior. Freud suggested that by identifying with his father's moral standards, which are all directed toward promotion and security of civilization, the boy develops a superego—the moral conscience.

More contemporary theorists have suggested that the Oedipal complex not only represents a pivotal point in the father-son dyad but also has a significant impact on how the boy begins to see and feel about the opposite sex. For instance, before the Oedipal complex is resolved the boy employs something called *psychic spitting* when thinking of his mother. He sometimes views her as the Madonna—the saintly mother who deserves his praise and adoration and to whom he freely gives loving affection—and then, at other times, he views her as the whore—the pejorative depository of sexual feelings. According to these theorists, until the Oedipal complex is resolved the boy cannot regard a woman with simultaneous sexual and tender feelings.

It is important to underscore the notion that Freud's writings on male sexuality can also be construed as a socially constructed form of myth. Just like other myths, they are created on a cultural level in an attempt to negotiate tensions that need to be worked out. In this case they serve many functions, including transitioning Western culture from the Victorian era to more contemporary conceptions of sexuality.

Disidentification

Building upon sexology and Freudian myth, later analytic theorists carried forward the notion that in order to become a proper man a boy needs to break away from emotional dependence and then receive instruction from an older man. Traditional psychoanalytic theory addresses masculine identity development, that is, how boys become men, by positing a process of disidentification. In a classic paper written by psychoanalyst Ralph Greenson (1968), disidentification is described as a two-pronged process whereby (1) a boy must renounce emotional ties to his primary caregiver (traditionally held to be his mother), and (2) he must counteridentify with his father or another male role model. These developmental tasks are held as necessary steps toward emotional and physical autonomy as well as being necessary for proper gender-identity development.

Greenson's (1968) first developmental step in the scheme of disidentification emphasizes the need for the maturing young male to progressively assume a greater sense of emotional and psychological separation from his female caregiver. This has come to mean that those things associated with the primary caregiving relationship, such as emotional dependence, vulnerability, and relational connection, must be renounced (Blazina, 1997). Those qualities are seen as having potential for corrupting the development of proper (stereotypical) masculinity.

Greenson's (1968) second step, which is interrelated with the first, is to have the boy counteridentify with his father. The male role model is needed to guide the male neophyte to avoid the pitfalls of femininity; otherwise the masculine self would be thwarted and unrealized. This guidance is provided by a father figure, male role model, or mentor who teaches the boy both how to be a man through exposure to traditional masculine behavior and how to avoid those activities and behaviors thought to be feminine (e.g., crying when hurt).

In addition to giving the boy a model for proper masculine identity, the father's role takes on another meaning. Horner (1984) has suggested that the role of the father in this developmental task is also to lure the child away from the maternal symbiotic relationship. Mahler and Gosliner (1955) have suggested that the father is important in terms of providing the necessary support needed to avoid reengulfment on the part of the mother. Abelin (1971) has suggested that the mother becomes associated with safety and a home base while the father represents a "non-mother" space related to exploration. Similarly, Meerloo (1968) has described the father as a bridge to the outside world. We see, then, in traditional analytic mythic paradigm that the mother comes to represent a potential danger that may cause the boy to lose his masculine identity, whereas the father is the means for his escape into manhood.

In a similar vein, Chodorow (1978) argues that boys face special developmental challenges as they proceed through the separation/individuation process because masculinity is based not upon a positive identification with the father but, rather, upon a negating of the relationship with the mother. Chodorow also suggests that boys face a special developmental task in disidentification in that they must define themselves as "not mom" and "not female." There must be a clear separation from the mother both intrapsychicly and interpersonally in order for a boy to adopt a masculine identity. According to Chodorow, "learning to be masculine comes to mean learning not to be womanly" (p. 109).

This original disidentification model has been criticized by proponents of competing contemporary mythic models of masculinity on several grounds. Among these criticisms is the contention that the boy is asked to psychologically separate from his caregivers much earlier than he is emotionally ready to do so (Betcher & Pollack, 1993; Pollack, 1995, 1998). While disidentification was traditionally held to represent the earliest steps toward masculine independence, contemporary theorists have suggested that it may actually result in a normative gender-specific developmental trauma due to maternal and paternal disconnection (Betcher & Pollack, 1993; Pollack, 1995). That is, boys at a young age are not emotionally equipped to survive on their own any more than girls are, but gender socialization forces them to do so prematurely, with damaging results. Pollack (1998) argues that premature psychological separation can occur even with well-intentioned caregivers (both male and female) and leads to emotional hardening and psychological maladjustment. Blazina (1997) suggests that the male child might be encouraged to break free of symbiosis in order to explore the world without being able to use the emotional tools he has internalized in his first encounter with objects. Further, the disidentification process may be a symbolic way to renounce many of the positive characteristics associated with this earliest relationship, including emotional connection, vulnerability, and the need for emotional nurturing.

The emergence of the disidentification process as the cornerstone of masculine development is a prime example of the evolution of the cultural myth of masculinity in process. While disidentification is a contemporary theme, it has its roots in the hero stories of Indo-European mythology. We see the Indo-European hero as one who must break free of the safety of the community to do battle with demons, dragons, monsters, and the like in order to reach the goal of being a successful warrior who has achieved the fame that does not decay. There is an emphasis upon valor. Breaking free of the safety of maternal care allows for the seeking of a male mentor who will infuse the neophyte with masculine virtues. This theme is recycled as the backdrop for the successful masculine neophyte who must now do battle with dangers of a different kind—engulfment by caregivers. In this case, hero status is the achievement of successful masculine identity through emotional independence and psychological separation. Whether we approach these hero's journeys from an objective perspective or engage the passionate pleas of advocates for a kinder, gentler way to raise boys, we are witness to how this part of the masculine paradigm has remained in the forefront of discussions of masculine identity.

FEAR OF THE FEMININE

Given that both mythic paradigms of sexology and psychoanalysis stressed genetic and social factors in the development of appropriate and inappropriate gender identity and sexual desire, it would seem reasonable that the gender-role models they proposed would also focus upon the descriptive and prescriptive notions of what is normal and abnormal. Central to the twentieth-century definition of normal male identity is the notion that stereotypical feminine behaviors and attitudes are a corrupting force. Blazina (1997) has noted that the fear of the feminine seems to have historical roots that can be found as far back as ancient Greece. Exactly what gets labeled as feminine and, consequently, what needs to be avoided seem to have evolved over time. Looking back to the ancient Greeks, for instance, we can see bands of fierce warriors who had same-sex relations, and in his *Symposium* Plato states that love between men "is the highest and noblest form." Further, sexual relations between men were viewed as an experience that intensified masculinity because it left women out of the equation. At the same time, there were firm taboos against boys' engaging in feminine behavior past puberty. Before then it was gender-appropriate to act out these feminine mannerisms. Considering the evolution of what is considered feminine and the twentieth-century fear of the feminine, these historical examples stand in stark contrast to the disdain for the same-sex relations of the sexual invert of sexology. What is meant by feminine has cultural and time-specific variations, but it is always seen as behavior that ultimately belongs within the realm of women, not men.

We can see the roots of the contemporary fear of the feminine in psychoanalytic psychology that stresses the engulfing powers of the mother in the disidentification process. Psychoanalytic writer Karen Horney (1932) has suggested that boys fear the engulfment of women if their symbolic phallic masculinity is found wanting. For Horney, men's sense of masculine identity wavered, never quite being on solid ground. Men were left with two options to protect and bolster themselves: to distance themselves from the feminine, or to engage in hypermasculine behavior as a way of compensating for a failing sense of masculinity. She has suggested that a dread of the feminine drives many stereotypical masculine behaviors. Dinerstein (1976) has taken this dynamic further in attempting to explain aspects of misogyny. She has argued that since the Industrial Revolution women have become more responsible for raising boys. This has caused women to become the targets of male aggression because they make the rules by which boys live and which they feel powerless to overthrow. This leaves emotional residual that is acted out in adulthood, as men may attempt to set the score straight through misogynistic acts.

Other theorists and researchers of the twentieth century have observed that men often experience discomfort with what is now considered the feminine. Jung (1953, 1954) has suggested the anima archetype to represent the feminine side of men, which they have difficulty integrating into their psyches. Levinson, Darrow, Klien, Levinson, and McKee (1978), have suggested that men view feminine parts of themselves as dangerous and try to neglect or repress them. McCreary (1994) has suggested that boys and men are dealt with more harshly than girls and women when they deviate from traditional societal gender-role prescriptions and therefore feel inclined to avoid the feminine. Pollack (1998) has suggested that, in keeping with teaching boys to avoid the feminine, many well-intentioned caregivers (both male and female) impose restrictive gender rules on their sons believing they are doing the right thing in terms of making their sons proper men. Osherson (1986), for instance, has painted the all-too-familiar scene of the distressed little boy crying out for emotional soothing only to encounter the minimizing of his pain. Solt (1996) has noted that the boy seeks validation especially from his male caregiver in terms of being a worthy member in the masculine world. He wants to be validated by the father as having an abundance of masculine traits and, by default, few or no feminine ones. When the child feels as though he does not meet this standard, his resulting anger is turned back on himself, damaging and potentially fragmenting his own psychological structure.

Psychoanalyst Greenson (1968) has posed a series of important questions regarding the feminine aspects of the mother to which the boy is exposed in the course of his initial psychological development into a man:

> What happens to the original identification with mother after the boy has identified with father? Does the identification with mother disappear, its place taken by the new identification with father? How much of the boy's identification with the father is a "contra"-identification? (p. 373)

Greenson is wondering here what happens to these banished traits of femininity after the boy solidifies his masculine identity. Blazina (1997) suggests that boys learn to separate themselves from them by "the feminine projection process" (p. 63). In this situation, men make clear demarcations, that these unwanted traits belong in the feminine realm and not within themselves. That is, by projecting these characteristics onto others (women and effeminate men), they feel free of the conflict about having the characteristics themselves. This is a temporary remedy, of course, because in moments of feeling vulnerable or less that perfectly powerful— in short, unstereotypically masculine—they will feel pressed to reclaim these disowned characteristics. This, in turn will call for even more stringent psychological defenses, such as the hypermasculine ones Horney (1932) suggested. In the long run this leads to a wavering sense of masculinity, one not firmly set or achieved. There is a certain irony in that both the disidentification process and the fear of the feminine strive to make men strong by removing what are considered weaker characteristics. Yet contemporary critics argue that this model of being a man actually impinges upon intrapsychic strength through imposing overly stringent standards (Blazina, 2001).

When following the cultural paradigm of male-identity development seen in nineteenth- and twentieth-century sexology and psychoanalysis, we see that sexual inversion, the fear of the feminine, and notions of male disidentification helped develop the resulting masculine myths. This mythos provides ideals to emulate and zanes to avoid.

GENDER IDENTITY MODEL

Lewis M. Terman and Catherine C. Miles's landmark book *Sex and Personality* (1936) helped incorporate the spirits of both psychoanalysis and sexology, evolving into what will be referred to as the Gender Identity Model (GIM)—the normative twentieth-century model of development for men and women. Echoing the earlier Freudian notion, in the GIM men and women grow into their proper roles guided by biological forces. This is, of course, in keeping with Krafft-Ebing's and Freud's emphasis upon biology's setting the tone for proper and unique gender specific development. Terman and Miles's (1936) thesis is presented here:

> The belief is all but universal that men and women as contrasting groups display characteristic sex differences in their behavior, and that these differences are so deep seated and pervasive as to lend distinctive character to the entire personality . . . but there is a growing tendency to concede equality or near equality with respect to general intelligence and the majority of special talents . . . the belief remains that sexes differ fundamental in their instinctual view and emotional equipment and in the sentiments, interests, attitudes, and modes of behavior, which are derivatives of such equipment. It will be recognized that there are important factors in shaping what is known as personality, hence the general acceptance of the dichotomy between the masculine and feminine personality types . . . the typical women is believed to differ from the typical man in the greater richness and variety of her emotional life. . . . In particular she is believed to experience in greater degree than the average man the tender emotions, including sympathy, pity, and parental love; to be more given to cherishing and protective behavior of all kinds. She is more religious and at the same time more prone to jealousy, suspicion, and injured feelings. Sexually she is by nature less promiscuous than man, is coy rather than aggressive, and her sexual feelings are less specifically located in her body. . . . Her moral life is shaped less by principles than by personal relationships, but thanks to her lack of adventurous nature she is much less subject than man to most types of criminal behavior. Her sentiments are more complex than man's and dispose her personality to refinement, gentility, and preoccupation with the artistic and cultural. (pp. 1–2)

We glean from this discussion several important points. The differences between men and women are "deep seated and pervasive," rooted in biology. These differences are to be understood in terms of a dichotomy—masculine versus feminine. Indeed, most of the descriptions of what men are revolve around what women are not and vise-versa. Some of the differences between women and men include the former's having more complex, richer emotional lives. Men instead are governed by a rational intellect.

It is interesting to note that the last edition of Terman and Miles's 1936 book was published in 1968. It shows the staying power of this theory and how it has been influential in shaping contemporary definitions of masculine and feminine. It represents a tangible expression of the cultural myth of masculinity in the twentieth century.

SEX-ROLE STRAIN AND GENDER-ROLE CONFLICT

Having examined the construction of the nineteenth–twentieth century hegemonic model of masculinity mythology as reflected in psychoanalysis and sexology, we go on to discuss notions of gender-role strain and conflict that arise in the waning of the twentieth century. Both sex-role strain and gender-role conflict underscore the new conflict many men in Western culture experience as they try to decide how to be a man. These conflicts are important on a sociocultural level because they highlight that fact that the hegemonic myth of masculinity is being challenged. The dominant model of masculinity may be waning in terms of levels of influence.

Joseph Pleck's book *The Myth of Masculinity* (1981) directly criticized the GIM and Terman and Miles (1936) for their assumption that biology rather than social forces created and shaped gender roles. In that work, Pleck suggests that the critique of the GIM could be condensed into three main criticisms: (1) there is an emphasis upon insecure or inadequate masculinity; (2) there are potential harmful consequences of a man's relationship with his mother; and (3) it views homosexuality as the worst condition that can befall a man. He suggests that these concepts are outdated and need to be reworked.

In contrast to the GIM, Pleck (1981) has offered his sex-role-strain theory, in which men are exposed to the impossible burden of living up to the strident demands of the GIM. The sex-role-strain model suggests that stereotypes and cultural norms define gender roles. This notion can be understood in terms of the hegemonic influence of the GIM. This dominant masculine paradigm will set a standard for the rest of the culture, and, in the case of the GIM, it is highly stringent and restrictive in terms of acceptable behavior.

Pleck (1981) has further argued that the stereotypical gender roles are not only impossible to live up to, but they impose psychological strain when they are not achieved. For instance, stereotypical conceptions of masculinity impose the dictum that a man must always be strong or keep his emotion in check. This is not possible and in many cases is not healthy for the individual; for example, when he experiences significant losses in life, when he is trying to form relationships, and so forth. Pleck has argued that when men do express emotions they experience a failure to achieve the GIM ideal and can suffer consequent social sanctions for violating stereotypical norms.

In a vein similar to Pleck's (1981) notion of sex-role strain, O'Neil, Helms, Gable, David, and Wrightsman (1986) have defined the notion of gender role conflict as "a psychological state where gender roles have negative consequences or impacts on a person or others" (p. 336). It has been hypothesized that the psychological undercurrent of this conflict or strain includes the fear and rejection of those qualities deemed feminine (O'Neil, 1982; O'Neil et al., 1986). According to O'Neil et al. (1986), the fear of the feminine helps define what is optimally masculine in Western culture, guiding the development of appropriate masculine gender roles by gauging and then rejecting those gender-specific behaviors considered to be traditionally within the feminine realm. O'Neil (1982) has defined this fear as "a strong, negative emotion in self or others associated with feminine values, attitudes, and behaviors" (p. 18). This includes but is not limited to emotional intimacy, vulnerability, and emotional dependency.

From O'Neil et al.'s (1986) theory came the development of the Gender Role Conflict Scale (GRCS). This instrument is correlated with measures of masculine ideology but is more focused upon the conflicts men experience when trying to adhere to them. It consists of thirty-seven statements concerning men's thoughts and feelings about gender-role behavior. There are four subscales: (1) success, power, competition; (2) restrictive emotionality; (3) restrictive affectionate behavior between men; and (4) conflict between work and family relations.

The GRCS has been a widely used measure for nearly twenty years and has shown a consistent relationship between men's gender-role conflict and psychological maladjustment including depression, anxiety, substance abuse, interpersonal problems, and so forth.

Both Pleck's (1981) and O'Neil et al.'s (1986) paradigms point toward the reconsideration of the hegemonic model of masculinity in the twentieth century. Certainly central to the new paradigm is more gender-role freedom for men. Pleck, Sonenstein, and Ku (1993) have suggested that "one must not speak of masculine, but only of masculinities" (p. 90). This points to a denial of the proposition that there is only one correct standard of masculinity to follow, with all others viewed as potential zanes. As gender-role reexamination continues, this new mythos may leave more room for the development and implementation of what had been considered nontraditional masculine coping skills alongside the more functional traditional ones. Psychologist Ronald Levant (1992) has suggested celebrating those areas of the traditional role that are valuable and worthwhile (e.g., the ability to think logically; being assertive; sacrificing one's own needs for the sake of the family; dedication, loyalty, and commitment) while building anew in those areas that are dysfunctional (e.g., funneling all negative emotion into anger, alexithymia, which is a severely limited experience or range of affect, and difficulty with emotional intimacy).

CURRENT AND COMPETING MASCULINE PARADIGMS

As the GIM wanes in terms of influence and as notions of gender-role conflict come to the fore, the dialectic process allows other models of masculinity to be potential challengers. This set of current cultural paradigms of masculinity serves both descriptive and prescriptive functions as it offers differing ways that men may conduct themselves. Currently there are coexisting and competing models for the template men should follow. One would expect there to be differing cultural myths based upon differing social classes, time periods, cultures, and so forth. For instance, scholars have recently challenged the notion that Victorian masculinity was the only masculine standard of the time period. Instead, there seem to have been a variety of competing models during that time period (Carnes & Griffen, 1990). Where we may differ from earlier times is in the sheer number of competing models that exist in contemporary Western society (Pendergast, 2000). This in itself may suggest that the evolution of masculinity has entered a fluid stage of expansion wherein more masculinities are perhaps both available and acceptable. Another possible explanation is that with increased scholarship we become more aware of factions of masculinity that are different from the hegemonic one. For instance, Clatterbaugh (1998) has suggested that by the close of the twentieth century there were at least eight different factions within the growing men's movement. Each competed for expression, and each offered descriptive and prescriptive aspects for how men should be. Each of these perspectives is briefly reviewed below. Again, I remind the reader that, just as with sexology and psychoanalysis, these are socially constructed notions of masculine paradigms. Their followers too may embrace the models discussed here as providing object truth for how men should live.

The Conservative Perspective

The conservative perspective honors traditional social and institutional values, which include the division of labor based upon gender. Men are the protectors and the providers and are dominant in business, politics, and other aspects of the public sphere. Women, on the other hand, are dominant in the private sphere and are responsible for family and care-giving. Violation of these codes is regarded as leading to social unraveling and moral upheaval.

Another faction within this perspective is that of the biological conservatives, who stress the influence of genetic predisposition in shaping gender identity and roles. That is, men and women have natures that are the result of biological influences. Thus, if men dominate the public sphere and women the private, it is not because of tradition but is due to biology's influencing social behavior.

The Profeminist Perspective

The profeminists reject the notion of biology or social convention and focus instead upon concepts of masculinity's having been created in order to sustain the privileges bestowed upon men. This social dynamic leads to the oppression of women (but allows for men's being harmed by it as well).

Within this perspective are the radical profeminists, who believe patriarchy is responsible for misogyny and the oppression of women. They maintain that patriarchy must be overthrown and replaced by feminist values that would lead to a society governed by noncompetitive and non-hierarchical mores.

The liberal profeminists comprise a third profeminist perspective, which argues that restrictive gender roles harm men and women alike. They maintain that both genders need to focus upon becoming fully human and free from social constraint. This model parallels the liberal women's movement represented by the National Organization for Women (NOW).

The Men's Rights Perspective

The advocates of the men's rights approach to masculinity hold that men are the targets of numerous psychological, legal, and social injustices, many of which go unrecognized or unacknowledged. By merging the father's rights movement with a political agenda for men, they attempt to act as advocates for men in various arenas. A strong focus of their activities is the political movement for fathers who do not receive equal and fair treatment in matters of divorce and child custody. They counter the argument that men enjoy a special status of privilege by maintaining that, quite to the contrary, males are the targets of a new sexism. This may take the form of a reverse sexism, wherein privilege and power do not always belong to men. Warren Farrell, for instance, has suggested, "It is in the area of physical health and longevity that men's power . . . begins to fall considerably short of women's power. There can be no greater loss of power than loss of life" (1987, p. 87).

The Mythopoetic Movement

The mythopoetic movement represents a neo-Jungian approach and maintains that masculinities derive from deep unconscious or archetypal sources. It maintains that the source of masculinity is best tapped through stories, myths, and rituals. Jungian analyst Robert Johnson (1974) has contributed much in this area, but perhaps best known is the poet Robert Bly, whose book *Iron John* (1990) focuses upon the need to incorporate the "deep" masculine back into the psyches of overfeminized men. Other writers in this area include Moore and Gillette (1991) and Michael Meade (1993). All proponents of this approach are in agreement that there has been a devastating (or distressing) absence of the father from the home since the Industrial Revolution. The presence of the father in preindustrial times allowed for a son to learn about the deep masculine firsthand. With the father absent, the boy is left feeling adrift in terms of how to be a man. A splinter mythopoetic group, the New Warrior movement (its members have recently changed their name to the Way of the Peaceful Warrior), emphasizes male initiation rituals into the deep masculine and conducts these rites in a wilderness setting.

Another subgroup of the mythopoetic movement, led by John Rowan, emphasizes the idea that masculinity is underfeminized. He uses the mythology of the great goddess to incorporate the feminine into men's lives. This viewpoint differs radically from that of the other mythopoetic approaches in advocating an openly humanistic and feminist perspective. For instance, in his 1987 work *Horned God,* Rowan argues that men need to learn to relate to the feminine and that initiation into manhood comes through connection with women, not men. That is, women will teach male neophytes how to be a man in a new and different way. From this, a new way of relating will transpire: "The new hero will not be clad in armor, and he will flow around adversaries rather than stand and fight" (p. 25).

The Socialist Perspective

Socialists argue that masculinity is built upon three ideas: (1) masculinity is shaped and created by class structure; (2) the ultimate cost of current concepts of masculinity is restricted potential for men; and

(3) concepts of masculinity can not change until the underlying class structure of society is altered. They maintain that a limited few—the owners of land and of the means of production—reap the benefits of society. The workers are oppressed in this process. The workingman's brand of masculinity enables him to feel solidarity with his working-class brethren and thereby resist the authority of the owning class. At the same time, oppressive social processes lead the workingman to feel alienated from himself, his family, and others. The aim, then, of the socialist perspective is to recreate a society of equality that includes equal shares for all men and women. This includes the owners and those who work for them. The notion of redistribution must take into account everyone. Only then will a new brand of masculinity, free from power and wealth, emerge.

The Gay Male Perspective

Part of the gay male perspective involves wrestling with the hegemonic masculinity's notion that homosexuality represents a feminized and thwarted masculinity. As mentioned previously, sexology, psychoanalysis, and gender-role paradigms helped promote the notion that homosexuality represented a contaminated masculinity. In contrast to this, the gay male perspective argues for a reconsideration of traditional notions of what is masculine and what is feminine. In the words of Dennis Altman, "In many ways we represent the most blatant challenge of all to the mores of a society organized around belief in the nuclear family and sharply differentiated gender roles" (1972, p. 56). Gay men must take on multiple roles as they act as caregivers, parents, community members, and significant others. Many of these roles cross the divide formerly placed between the genders and challenge the notion that gay masculinity is an oxymoron. This faction calls the hegemonic notion of masculinity into question and forces a rethinking of gender roles.

The African American Perspective

Many writings of the men's movement place an emphasis upon people of European descent. The African American perspective has been at the forefront of proposing alternate paradigms of masculinity for those of other ethnic backgrounds. Writers in this area contend that black men have faced and continue to face a unique set of difficulties whose origins can be found in societal and historical roots. When considering themselves in relation to the hegemonic masculinity, many African American men feel left out (Franklin, 1994a). "Understanding Black men means recognizing that in America adult Black males have been Black 'men' for only about twenty years. In addition, even during this time Black males have not been recognized as 'societally approved' men" (Franklin, 1994a, p. 275).

Confronted with a number of oppressive societal dynamics, such as racism, crime, poverty, and lack of employment, black men have responded with their own brand of masculinity. For instance, Franklin (1994b) has suggested that black men may adopt a conformist masculinity and try to emulate the hegemonic model's behavior and attitudes. They may also adopt a ritualistic model, much like the conformist model. However, they are different in that they do not really believe in the hegemonic rules and institutions yet still play the game.

There are other, less traditional models of black masculinity. Innovative black masculinity abandons conformity and ritualistic paradigms. Instead, it may incorporate aspects of hegemonic masculinity and exaggerate them. For instance, an abasement of women occurs in rapper and gangster attitudes. Retreatist black masculinity gives up any hope of success and falls into despair, addiction, and homelessness.

The Promise Keepers

The Evangelical Christian movement known as the Promise Keepers emphasizes the literal interpretation of the Bible as the model for masculinity. As Jesus was to the Christian church, so should men be to their families. They should be leaders, protectors, and providers. The main focus of this movement is to acknowledge that men have not always done these things well in the past and that a personal relationship with Jesus will help men to lead their families and be men of God.

CONCLUSION

In this chapter, we have focused upon the powerful interplay between sexology, psychoanalysis, and gender-role paradigms in the construction of the myth of masculinity in the nineteenth and twentieth centuries. When these various approaches are examined together, the picture becomes clear regarding the cumulative impact of each of these interrelated disciplines upon conceptions of masculinity. A central aspect of the resulting mythos is that masculine identity is seen as a developmental process whereby the achievement of preconceived standards of thought and behavior is a marker for masculine health. For instance, in the psychoanalytic notion of the disidentification process, a boy must follow prescribed steps in order to achieve a masculine identity. If the steps are interrupted along the way or goals are not achieved, the attainment of a positive masculine identity can easily be corrupted or thwarted. The most likely culprit in this corrupting process is that which was considered stereotypically feminine during the time period.

Just as we have seen the fluid nature of the definition of masculinity, so we must take into account changes in conceptions of what is considered feminine behavior. During most of the nineteenth and twentieth centuries, masculine and feminine were viewed as divergent constructs that occupied opposite ends of a gender continuum. Thus, Terman and Miles's discussion in 1936 of the differences between men and women in a mutually exclusive fashion in their book *Sex and Personality* is reflective of the time period. Men are men and women are women, and never the two shall occupy the same space. We could examine differing threads taken from sexology, psychoanalysis, and gender-role paradigms in order to understand what these approaches viewed as being the destructive aspects of the feminine that thwart masculinity. These differing aspects include showing vulnerability, assuming a passive stance, needing others, experiencing gender-role ambiguity, and making decisions based on emotion instead of reason.

What may be concluded is that the warrior ethic seems to be a critical root for the making of the GIM of the twentieth century. It has already been noted that the militarization of masculinity had become a guiding force for the new middle class. Those aspects that nineteenth- and twentieth-century masculinity deemed feminine are seen as corrupting forces within this ethic. At the same time, the other masculinity of the refined nobleman also was present and influenced the upper-middle-class definition of masculinity. It was seen (as in the Middle Ages) as a reflection of higher social standing and the proof of being others' betters.

It was only later that the corrupting notion of the feminine was changed, when Jung (1953, 1954) argued for a more integrated perspective wherein a man by his very nature is masculine but, in order to be a whole, healthy individual, also needs to incorporate characteristics deemed as feminine into his personality. Still later, in the 1970s, gender-role theorist Sandra Bem (1974) suggested that the old ways of conceptualizing masculine and feminine were outdated and needed to be replaced with what she called "instrumental" and "expressive" aspects of personality. This, she maintained would allow both men and women to have a mix of both personality characteristics that she termed "psychological androgyny." This new concept for gender ideals, at least in the field of psychology, allows for men to be valued for being more emotionally integrated. One can see what a vast departure that is from sexology's earlier notion of sexual inversion whereby a man can be labeled deviant simply for not always assuming the dominant role in his romantic relationships.

This new integrated perspective that has been embraced by some factions within psychology does not necessarily find its way to prominence as the dominant social paradigm of masculinity (although it is a clear indication that the concept of the masculine ideal is in a state of flux). Rather, this integrated notion of masculinity lies in wait as yet another potential competitor among the various masculine paradigms that Clatterbaugh (1998) has mentioned.

We can speculate that this paradigm of a new, emotionally integrated male is a new attempt at solving an old cultural riddle. The two masculinities represented in the Indo-European culture of warrior versus aristocracy are echoed in both Jung's (1953, 1954) and Bem's (1974) ideal man. This ideal man is asked to straddle the worlds that are separated by the class distinctions in regard to masculinity that we have previously seen in the Middle Ages and then, later, in the making of the modern middle class. This ideal man incorporates the refinement of the aristocratic tradition. However, there is now special emphasis upon characteristics such as emotional awareness and being in touch with his feminine side. At the same time, he is a man's man incorporating the valor of the warrior caste.

While this is a new take on an old mythic paradigm, it (or perhaps some derivation of it) stands as the one model that may best fit Indo-European culture. It attempts to incorporate elements from what have been the dominant castes throughout Western culture—the warriors and the aristocracy. In short, to combine these two castes in some workable form meets the requirements of Western culture's ideal man. In theory, the king or ruler in an Indo-European culture exemplified and symbolized the divergent aspects of his people. His power rested on the notion that he embodied and represented all that he ruled. This might also include representing the varying notions of masculinities expressed in his culture. In this way, the integrated man—or some derivation of that concept—appears to very closely reflect a conglomerate of the Indo-European male ideal. This includes both notions of an ideal man, such as a workable combination of valor and nobility, and how those notions get translated into a more concrete paradigm of an ideal man. This is reflected in more contemporary interpretations of this Indo-European paradigm in the works of such theorists as Jung (1953, 1954) and Bem (1974).

If it is the case that the integrated warrior/aristocrat model is closest to the Indo-European ideal, why has it not risen to prominence as the hegemonic model of masculinity? We as a culture move through periods in which we temporarily favor one of the two masculinities over the other.

We have war and peacetime leaders and heroes that fall in and out of favor. But, living in an Indo-European culture, we eventually have to account for both paradigms. This may be why the notion of somehow joining these two seemingly divergent paradigms continues to reemerge throughout the history of Western culture. We see this joining in the noble knight and in psychology's integrated man. However, to find a satisfying and workable melding of the two masculinities is, to say the least, a difficult task.

Our examination of myth has suggested that on a cultural level we have been attempting some integration of this material for some time. It is difficult to determine whether this has to do with some psychological need, as Jung (1953, 1954) would argue, or whether it represents a pragmatic solution for a culture that favors the ideals of both warrior and aristocratic masculinity. In either case, when a real individual or some mythic expression of one is able to capture aspects of both masculinities well, he is met with acceptance and adoration. However, when this integration is not accomplished well, he may be at risk for being labeled a zane. In short, it is difficult enough to master one of the masculinities levels, much less incorporate both.

This notion of the integrated male's representing the Indo-European male ideal is contingent upon the idea that there is a continued hegemonic emphasis upon characteristics that represent the first two castes (i.e., warrior and aristocracy). However, to truly represent all aspects of the culture is also to include the characteristics represented by the third caste of the Indo-European culture. Can we assume that much of the contemporary notion of the third caste's masculine ideal is absorbed by and can be explained within the context of the other two masculinities? Probably not, but the degree to which there is a distinctness of the third caste and an intermingling of ideals among all castes will need to be examined with more research. For instance, some of the "new" masculine paradigms that Clatterbaugh has noted may have their roots in the everyday world of the third caste. This caste has its roots as the sustenance providers of ancient Indo-European culture, those who provided the platform on which the other two castes stood. If it is fair to transpose the tripartite social structure from the ancient world to contemporary times (this may be a discussion in and of itself), we can see that the third caste represents the "regular guys" of the working class. Do these regular Joes look to those above them on the social hierarchy when creating a masculine ideal, or do they have their own distinct notion of how to be a man? In reality, it is probably some combination of both.

In defining the masculine ideal of the third caste in more contemporary times, however, we expect many men to experience conflict when looking beyond the warrior prototype as a potential ideal. To go beyond this and begin emulating the nobleman is to put on an air that may move too far away from the working class's conception of masculinity. For many, this may be seen as a betrayal of one's social caste. A prime example of this can be seen in the life and times of Audie Murphy, the most decorated solider in U.S. history. This World War II hero, who was a dirt-poor farmer in Texas, rose through the ranks in the military based on his acts of valor. However, the mythos suggests he initially refused several attempts to be commissioned as an officer and, instead, wanted to stay at the highest rank for an enlisted man that was not referred to as "sir." To be called "sir" is to move into that aristocracy and betray the working class.

Then, there are those other regular Joes who grow up with working-class roots and through their success in sports (the peacetime version of being a warrior), education, or business (i.e., financial success) transcend the third caste. Some of these men attempt to emulate the aristocracy's notion of ideal masculinity. We see this in the mythos of F. Scott Fitzgerald's *Great Gatsby,* (1925) wherein a come-from-nothing man loses the girl of his dreams because he is poor and she is from the aristocracy. He is obsessed with putting as much distance as possible between himself and his humble upbringing.

Has the masculinity ideal of the third caste changed over time? Just as we suspect that there has been movement and flux in terms of definitions of masculinity in the first two castes, so we must draw the same conclusion with regard to the third division of Western culture. Ideal masculinities seem to change not only across the culture as a whole but also within its various subgroups. For instance, the masculine ideal that Dionysus may have represented at the inception of the third caste in Indo-European culture does not ring true in more contemporary times. What is retained at the core of the third-caste definition is an emphasis upon the productive force that carries the rest of the culture. However, there are variations in how this theme appears throughout the history of the third caste.

In regard to our understanding of masculinity on the mythic level, Clatterbaugh's (1998) discussion of the differing contemporary competing models of masculinity is important. At the beginning of this chapter, I argued that psychology's notion of manhood was a form of myth. While some factions of the men's movement may be reluctant to be considered under the umbrella of psychology (much less as a socially constructed form of myth), this overarching concept allows for the study of gender roles. Each of these models has its heroes and zanes; each has its own beliefs about what a man should be. Oftentimes their basic tenets are in direct contradiction with one another. Indeed, at times conflicts arise even within a faction. The intense fervor expressed by each faction's membership with regard to the right way men should be leads us back to the notion that these are all ultimately myths. They are socially constructed realities regarding various notions of ideal masculinity. There are sociocultural pressures that call new paradigms into being and cause others to be discredited.

However, with that said, contradiction does not undermine the role these models play—mythic or not—in giving various men of various beliefs a guide for ideal masculinity. These myths serve a needed function, offering cultural icons and methods of masculine socialization.

What is ultimately garnered from this mythic understanding of masculinity is the knowledge that we live inside our own paradigms of masculinity and see them as abject reality. It is often very difficult to see them any other way because the paradigm to which we belong serves some purpose or carries some meaning that makes it feel right or correct to us. The challenge is to know on one level that we can hold to our own paradigms but at the same time step outside of them for objective inspection. We must have the freedom to move into and out of socially constructed paradigms of masculinity for the sake of scholarship. This freedom is also important to men who are trying to discern what kind of masculinity they wish to embrace.

These descriptive and prescriptive perspectives on masculinity make clear that the hegemonic masculinity that enjoyed prominence through much of the twentieth century is being challenged. In keeping with the dialectic process that is the mechanism of cultural change, splinter groups have arisen to challenge the dominant paradigm of masculinity. This would also suggest that the next hegemonic evolution of masculinity is in the process of becoming.

Chapter 7

CONCLUSION

What should we draw from our examination of the cultural myth of masculinity? Pleck (1981) and Connell (1995) have maintained that at any given time there is one dominant paradigm of masculine ideals within a culture. In this work I have argued that these ideals are reflected in both the cultural icons that are embraced as heroes and gods and the models for male socialization that govern everyday notions of how men should be within a society. In short, we see these aspects reflected in the culture's mythic paradigms of masculine icons and its paradigms of socialization. Though I make an artificial division of these types of myths here, in fact they are often intertwined. Further, we can derive both descriptive and prescriptive aspects from these types of myth viewed as a whole. Sometimes a specific hero in a cherished story points toward an ideal for masculinity within the culture. At other times, what is viewed as proper masculinity is reflected in the paradigms of gender socialization and looked to as guides for the society. These templates are not always clear to the naked eye; rather, the cultural myth needs to be decomposed and deciphered for us to appreciate its full message. When doing this, we can see how the fabric of what is considered to be masculine is woven of many areas of culture, such as art, religion, and so forth.

This process of deciphering cultural dynamics enables us to take a more integrative approach to examining sociocultural forces that shape the construction of masculine ideals. It also provides a framework that allows areas of study previously held to be unrelated or divergent to interface.

This is important because a plethora of complex issues needs to be considered. When examining these seemingly divergent areas individually, we lose the cumulative effect of the many influences that have shaped modern society's views of masculinity. Sexology, psychoanalysis, the influence of the Judeo-Christian morality upon the warrior mentality, the rise of capitalism, the development of the middle class—all these factors form an interrelated weave within the fabric of our reality. Each strand forms a part of the texture, and each can be fully appreciated only when considered in the company of the others. Perhaps this holistic approach to the study of masculinity will begin a dialogue among gender theorists and, as Connell (1995) has suggested, enable them to look beyond gender in order to understand gender.

THE EVOLVING MYTH OF WESTERN MASCULINITY

The myth of masculinity has evolved over time, and current conceptions of masculinity are built upon earlier notions that once enjoyed hegemonic influence. To understand how this evolutionary process has brought us to contemporary notions of masculinity, it is important to highlight three prominent influences: (1) social-class definitions of masculinity among the Indo-European tripartite society (including the Indo-European warrior ethic and ruling aristocracy), (2) Western culture's longstanding confusion regarding the proper roles for men, and (3) ever-changing sociocultural issues (e.g., the economy), which constantly challenge current conceptions of masculinity. These overlapping concepts cannot be neatly separated from one another.

Initially, it is important to consider whether the tripartite structure of PIE culture can be applied to contemporary Western culture. This book has argued for contextual analysis of myth and social structure, and this same approach must be taken to answer this question. This analysis reveals that, while it may not be as neatly defined as, for example, the feudal systems of the Middle Ages, we can make a reasonable argument that this social system still permeates Western culture. However, like most myths or social structures, it has evolved over time to account for new cultural entities such as the birth of the middle class and the process of social mobility. We may still examine social membership in terms of Indo-European castes, but issues such as social permeability and changing membership make the analysis more complex. What is most important is that each caste does still seem to resonate with its own masculine ideal.

Western culture's original definition of masculinity can be traced back to its PIE roots—especially the PIE warrior ethic. The right and privilege to bear arms generated a class of warriors that placed strong emphasis upon maintaining one's honor as well as achieving the fame that does not decay. In this sense, the warrior's actions are directed toward glory, sometimes in his own self-interest and other times for the betterment of the community. The PIE warrior ethic finds expression (in its daughter languages and cultures) in the sagas and legends of heroes and zanes. Both heroes and zanes are important players in exemplifying the importance of the warrior ethic within the culture. We can even see aspects of this dynamic's extending its reach into frameworks of culture such as the Declaration of Independence and the Constitution of the United States. Not only are men created equal (a notion that flies in the face of class privilege), but the nonaristocracy has the right to bear arms, a privilege previously reserved for the warriors and the aristocracy. Middle-class men of the eighteenth century could now form militia to defend against foreign invaders or find a satisfaction of honor in the duel. Before the rise of the middle class, the exclusive right to bear arms was a privilege whose violation was punishable by law.

With the coming of Christianity, the Indo-European warrior was infused with Judeo-Christian ethics and purpose. We see this in the inception of the Holy Roman Empire, when kings and their retainers were placed in the position of defending Christendom. The new warrior ethic came to full flower as a new template for masculinity in the Middle Ages. Its warriors were in the service of Christ, building the fame that does not decay in the Christian heaven as well as on earth. While reward for service in this life as well as the next may not be a concept new to the Indo-European warrior, what is novel is the code of chivalry. This code takes the Indo-European warrior, who already values honor and courage, and adds a new moral compass. Mercy for the weak, helping widows and orphans, and, of course, aiding damsels in distress are added to the warrior's more complex template of proper masculine behavior.

While chivalry did not continue in its original form past the fifteenth century—knights on horseback jousting in shiny armor, and so forth— elements were maintained or later resurrected and reinvented. The knight-errant's wanderlust and need to explore continued, as did the importance of the old, hardened warrior ways of honor and courage. These were incorporated in some fashion within colonialism as the Spanish conquistadors and the rugged American frontiersmen set out for adventure in foreign lands. Though the adventure may have carried a chivalric twist, oftentimes their treatment of the natives these colonialists encountered lacked the same moral compass reserved for the defense of say, widows and orphans.

Later in the eighteenth and nineteenth centuries, the development of a new middle class led to a redefinition of masculinity. This new social class was in need of masculine icons, and the aristocratic/warrior castes of old were chosen. However, these traditional symbols of masculinity were revamped to accommodate middle-class needs. A gentleman could now be constructed from character alone (i.e., by behavior), with or without pedigree and aristocratic wealth. Furthermore, this new approach to masculinity was embellished by the rise of the romantic movement, which recycled old warrior icons from Nordic/Germanic/Celtic/Greek myths and added to their themes from the new conception of masculinity. The noble knight and similar heroes adorned the literature and educational materials of the day. They became implicit and explicit models for boys to emulate in order to become gentleman of character.

The birth of psychoanalysis and sexology caused a further evolution in the template of what was to become modern middle-class masculinity. Each contributed substantially to the creation of the GIM, which posited deep-seated and pervasive differences between men and women as the normative model for twentieth-century gender roles. Psychoanalysis would suggest that psychological health was defined by following nature's lead, in that the anatomical differences between men and women make for mutually exclusive categories of differing behaviors. Men are masculine and women are feminine, and because of their innate biological bases, these conditions are inevitable and irrevocable when considering proper development. Sexology originally referred to the study of sexual variations and the defining of a norm of sexual behavior. Its tenets were often used in a divisive fashion to create sexual zanes, that is, men who did not follow the norm. Its term *sexual inverts* usually referred to homosexuals and other men who did not match the cultural hegemonic myth of masculinity. If one could not be categorized as a rugged individualist, a muscular Christian, a captain of industry, a landowner, or the like, he was in jeopardy of being labeled a sexual invert.

The warrior ethic seems to be the critical root of the GIM of the twentieth century as that model attempted to define acceptable masculine behaviors in the middle class. The warrior ethic also allowed for a fair amount of social mobility in building the middle class. While much glory can be and has been attributed to this ethic, the contemporary cultural paradigm challenges the warrior lifestyle. In tales and legends, the emotionless warrior can stand blood-soaked in battle and not blink an eye. His composure is such that he can make a clever quip before he himself dies or before he takes the life of his foe. However, contemporary reinterpretation highlights the warrior's struggles to connect emotionally, show vulnerability, or have his life enriched by others. In the warrior ethic these are all signs and symptoms of weakness and are to be avoided. The more contemporary cultural myth asks him to reconsider his self-imposed isolation and to at least consider riding off into the sunset in the company of someone else.

While the warrior ethic is a prominent influence in the evolving myth of masculinity, the accompanying ruling aristocracy in the Indo-European tripartite structure must also be considered. As mentioned in chapter 1, this social class had differing rules for masculine behavior than did the warrior class. This is best reflected in Tacitus's writings about the ancient Germans, whose warriors were chosen on the basis of valor but whose rulers were chosen on the basis of nobility. This seems to be a prevalent theme in much of Indo-European culture. Rulers may theoretically have their roots in the warrior class and be supported by them, but at times they are so removed from the warrior ethic that they need a "true warrior" with whom to consult and, perhaps, even be mentored or rescued by. This ruling aristocracy paradigm would suggest a differing code of masculinity. One illustration of this is the ornate splendor of the nobility in the medieval chivalry tales. This ornate external appearance is supposed to reflect the man's internal order and reflect a higher, more refined evolution of the individual. To be too closely associated with the bellicosity of the warrior class might show a lack of refinement.

Our examination of male norms reveals an ongoing tension and confusion that accompanies the nineteenth and twentieth centuries' middle-class definitions of masculinity. This men's role confusion has ancient roots and is part of what the modern middle-class man inherits when he attempts to use earlier class paradigms as a model for his own masculinity. We see male confusion clearly in the tension between the Indo-European and the pre-Hellenic (earth goddess) cultures, which came together to produce classical Greek mythology. We also see this in the competing models of masculinity in the Middle Ages—the old warrior ethic versus the courtly revision of tight tunics and curled hair.

Further difficulty and tension occurs when class distinctions of masculinity become too closely blended. For instance, the warrior in the Middle Ages was placed in beautiful adornment that was supposed to reflect internal order and the higher evolution of the aristocracy. This emphasis seems to challenge the old ways of the hardened and battle-tested warrior. A warrior in the new paradigm was supposed to be a gentleman with courtly refinement and bear arms. While an examination of cultural myths reflects an attempt to resolve this tension between warrior and gentleman, a final workable solution is not found.

With the later creation of the middle class, these males of the new social entity inherited similar troubling choices with regard to how to resolve matters of valor and nobility. Which paradigm should they emulate? The warrior/valor ethic seems to resonate in the American cowboy, the frontiersman, and the rugged individualist of the nineteenth and twentieth centuries. The medieval masculinity of the ruling/upper class (an ethic now open to members of the middle class) is more aligned with the essence of the courtly gentleman. The tripartite Indo-European paradigm, which had differing definitions of masculinity based upon different functions within the community, now causes confusion in the new middle class. Middle-class masculinity can be corrupted by forces that lie outside the warrior ethic, those more closely associated with the refinement of the ruling aristocracy. Perhaps this is in part what theorists like Pleck (1981) and O'Neil (1982) are referring to when they discuss gender-role strain or conflict. Men of the middle class are confused about which paradigm to adopt.

Adding to their confusion, nineteenth- and twentieth-century sexology, psychoanalysis, and gender-role paradigms placed heavy emphasis upon what men should not be; that is, these paradigms identify the cultural zanes. These include sexual inverts, of which the most notorious are gay men. There are also men (homosexual and heterosexual alike) who are too closely tied to notions of the feminine, be it personified as a mother figure or merely the characteristics associated with her. In more recent times, these paradigms are founding wanting, placing more emphasis upon what men should not be than upon what model to follow. Clatterbaugh (1998) identifies other contemporary paradigms of masculinity that strive for a more prescriptive approach to masculinity and consequently fill this void. Men are given a number of models from which to choose, and, as would be expected, these paradigms are in competition and sometimes directly contradict one another in terms of describing how men should be. On the one hand, it is suggested that men incorporate the "wild man" and the "deep masculine." On the other, they are told that traditional masculine qualities lead to patriarchy and suppression of the rights of others. Still others suggest that it is the duty of men to lead their families in spiritual matters, while most of these models emphasize a relational context and suggest that men should connect emotionally with significant others. The personal determination of which model to follow can be a confusing and difficult process.

What must be considered here is the complexity of the twentieth century, which caused the dialectic process of changes in masculinity to enter a new era. Since the "war of the functions" (Dumézil, 1970, 1973) wherein earth goddess culture interfaced with Indo-European culture, Western paradigms of masculinity have enjoyed single combat for the dominant notion of masculine ideals. That is, only the two masculinities (i.e., the warrior and the aristocrat paradigms) have competed against each other. This seems due in part to the fact that rigid notions of social class allowed only those paradigms that came from the aristocracy or warrior caste to be dominant. However, in the latter part of the twentieth century, sociocultural forces such as the feminist movement, more latitude for tolerance of diversity, and more or less prolonged economic and political prosperity led to a plethora of masculine paradigms' being thrown into the social mix. Paradigms that might have been dismissed previously due to the overwhelming acceptance of a current hegemonic model rose up to challenge its dominant place. Some of these paradigms may have their roots in the third caste of the Indo-European culture—the sustenance providers.

A contextual analysis of the masculine ideal would suggest that in the battle of the functions Indo-European culture interfaced with an earth goddess culture. One could reasonably assume that this culture had its own gender rules and ideals that were in some ways vastly different from the Indo-European's. For instance, Eisler (1988) has suggested that this earth goddess culture was more peacelike in nature and valued more gender equality. These cultural ideals had implications for not only the women of the culture but also for its men, even if the culture had a matrifocal sociocultural structure. As this culture intermingled with and was overtaken by the Indo-Europeans, its members were labeled as sustenance providers and driven to the lowest caste of the social structure. As one might suspect, the cultural ideals taken from the subservient third caste were dismissed by the first two castes. This dismissal includes the earth goddess culture's notions of masculine ideals. So we may speculate that what once may have been the hegemonic masculine ideal of an earth goddess culture found itself dismissed as a paradigm in the new Indo-European social context. Further, we would expect there to be an evolution of the masculine ideal of the third caste under the new Indo-European influence. As argued previously, with the rise of the middle class this may eventually have included the incorporation of the notions of the warrior ethic into the third caste's definition of masculinity.

Sustenance provider masculinity seems to have been held in check by the two masculinities over the course of Western cultural evolution until near the end of the twentieth century. It is the social permeability that is distinct to Western culture, especially in the United States, that allows this other masculinity (along with other paradigms) to be considered as viable alternatives to the hegemonic ideal. In the United States, a mythology that is tightly interwoven with the nation's identity allows for any schoolchild to grow up to become president of the country. There was a notion of social permeability in the ancient Indo-European culture based on deeds of valor, but even with this an allotted number of generations had to pass before one's family was recognized as belonging to the nobility. The stories of nineteenth-century author Horatio Alger, who wrote many books for boys that remained popular into the early twentieth century, reflect a mythos that theoretically allows much quicker movement across castes. It also allows the hero to come from less-than-noble stock. It is his behavior that transcends his social standing and elevates him.

But how distinct are this sustenance-provider masculinity and the other potential new paradigms from the two masculinities that are the foundation of the Indo-European culture? Can the lines that differentiate the caste ideals for masculinity be drawn so neatly? Are there aspects in the newer paradigms of masculinity that cross the boundaries of caste? More scholarship is needed to answer these questions. Suffice it to say that little in sociocultural studies is neatly explained. I offer the Indo-European and its tripartite frameworks as models that seem to have potential for explaining some of the sociocultural forces at work in Western culture and as a starting point for more integrated studies of masculinity.

CURRENT STATE OF MASCULINITY

In order to begin these investigations, I will briefly explain how the various traditional conceptions impact current notions of masculinity. The introductions of these alternatives for the masculine ideal (the sustenance provider or other paradigms) have naturally led to a period of unrest and uncertainty for many men. Which paradigm(s) should they emulate? Which one(s) should they teach to their sons? Decisions were confusing enough when there was just the choice between two masculinities.

Scholars have noted that we are in a crisis in regard to masculinity (Levant, 1992; Horrocks, 1994). I would agree with them to a certain degree. However, I do not view this crisis as a negative happening. Rather, the crisis we face is simply indicative of a new mix of sociocultural elements that in turn leads to a new set of ambiguities and complexities related to gender. In short, there are new mythic rules to play by, and their accompanying objectives may be altered. Thus, when I speak of masculine crisis I am referring to the shifting or blending of paradigms, not to a negative sociocultural phenomenon.

It also is important to determine whether this crisis represents a momentary shift away from the two masculinities or is a legitimate development toward a new paradigm of masculinity in Western culture. In regard to the changing nature of masculinity, we must consider shifts of the favored paradigm of the moment (e.g., warrior versus aristocrat) as cultural changes on the microlevel. We can see historically that the favored son moves back and forth across time. We can also see that the creation of a new paradigm of masculinity—as with the development of chivalry, the struggles of the ancient Greeks, or the making of the middle-class notion of one—occurred in periods when there was a crisis on a larger level in regard to gender issues. To study these micro- and macrolevels of change reaffirms the idea that similar types of crises have been dealt with before and that many of the clues as to how they were negotiated can be found in the mythic realm. Without this vital knowledge, there may be a natural fear that our current crisis of masculine identity represents a new phenomenon that cannot be successfully negotiated. While unnerving, the examination of the current crisis of masculinity may ultimately be about both the transition from one dominant paradigm of masculinity to another and how this process is occurring. To have so many potential paradigms competing at once may be straining both the dialectic process and the men who are looking for clear answers as to how they should conduct themselves. We can only wait and see the end result of the current mythos of diversity. Any time there is significant movement on the sociocultural level there is turmoil, and as cultural descendents of Apollo, the Indo-European god of light, we cherish clarity, not chaos.

Nonetheless, if our current period does represent the creation of a new paradigm of masculinity, we should look for the same sociocultural means at work that have been noted for millennia, that is, the use of myth as a tool to help lessen uncertainty in chaotic times. We should expect a new mythos to arise that helps bridge the gaps between paradigms and works through gender-role tensions on a cultural level. We will see these paradigms and works in plays, television shows, movies, literature, and art—in short, in the very fabric of our culture—until a new synthesis is brought to bear. There will emerge new mythic icons (probably borrowed in part from the past) that point men toward a solution. Accompanying these new heroes will be the socialization patterns that teach males the right way to be a man.

When considering the making of modern masculinity it is also imperative to take into account the importance of an ever-changing economy. While economics is certainly not the sole sociocultural factor in contemporary society, it is very important. As far back as the

Proto-Indo-Europeans, culture was heavily influenced by economy; in their case it was based upon cattle. Hero myths were constructed around men who could enhance themselves and their communities through economic means (e.g., the stealing and retrieval of cattle). There is even some support for the proposition that economy was one of the factors that influenced the Proto-Indo-Europeans to leave the steppes of eastern Russia. In the "long sixteenth" century (from about 1450 to 1650), when the advent of capitalism spurred the rise of the middle class, and again in the nineteenth and twentieth centuries, the economy was a powerful factor in determining the nature of masculine paradigms. With the influence of the Industrial Revolution, the turn-of-the-twentieth-century U.S. economy shifted from small, shop-based capitalism to a system based largely upon large-scale corporations (Pendergast, 2000). This occurred in the context of other forces such as an influx of immigration, increases in population density within urban areas, and a new availability of leisure time and activities. With this was a development within the middle class leading to the consumption of goods. All these social developments had a powerful impact upon male gender norms. The latter half of the nineteenth century had been marked by the prominence of Victorian masculinity based upon owning property (thereby assuring economic success), practicing self-control, and developing character. As middle-class men sought leisure and recreation in the new, twentieth-century period of consumerism, they found new venues for courtship and a new emphasis upon the body as a commodity that could be purchased (Highwater, 1991). In *The First Sexual Revolution,* White (1993) highlights the notion that the masculine ideal that emerged to replace the Victorian paradigm was one that valued appearance, personality, and sexuality.

THE SOCIALLY CONSTRUCTED CULTURAL MYTH OF MASCULINITY

The cultural myth of masculinity is a socially constructed paradigm. It carries with it the masculine ideals of a culture during a specific time period. The distance of history is an ally as it allows for a certain perspective when attempting to discern the foundation upon which our modern masculinity was built. That distance allows us to step outside our current cultural paradigms and examine cultural myths that reflected masculine ideals but not necessarily the reality of what men were or how they acted. For instance, history tells us that the crusaders did not always act in Christian fashion. King Richard the Lion-Hearted had more than 5,000 Saracens beheaded in one day. Chivalrous knights raped noble damsels as well as common folk, in anything but a chivalrous fashion. Victorian gentleman who valued their chastity did not count frequent visits to the brothel as staining their sense of purity as long as no one knew about them.

Thus we see that the historical inconsistency in mythic ideals does not detract from myth's socially constructed purpose to give order, predictability, and meaning to life. These same imperatives certainly apply to the conceptions of gender within contemporary Western culture. As long as the culture maintains a gendered sense of self, that is, a dichotomy of what gender-role behavior belongs in the realm of men versus that of women, we will need gender ideals. They guide us with regard to how we are supposed to conduct ourselves within the culture, given the specific sociocultural climate. Further, the masculine ideals that arise do so as a response to the specific sociocultural needs of the period. These resulting ideals can range from warrior to peace lover, from adventurer to settler, and from capitalist to king.

In the end, it is difficult from a scholastic perspective to pass critical judgment on those ideals that have come before or, more specifically, ones that do not match today's notions. A case in point is one of the central themes in men's studies, Why do men have such trouble connecting with others? While it is beyond the scope of this work to answer this question in depth, suffice it to say that historical sociocultural forces incorporated a mythology of masculinity that emphasized a stiff upper lip. Stretching back to the Indo-European ideal of the exploration of perilous foreign lands, the frontiersman notion of the Wild West, or our reaching into the vast darkness of outer space, the warrior ideal is more about action and less about reflection. It is a central part of the Western mentality to push on, to explore the unknown, and, as one famous starship captain put it, "to boldly go where no man has gone before." In many cases, the myths that we have examined here suggest that more interpersonal connections occur for men when they share this perilous journey. This sharing may range from the traditional warrior-type endeavors (i.e., going to war) to twentieth-century notions of masculine developmental theory wherein frightening notions of the feminine may push boys and men closer through what some have suggested as the trauma of being a male. Have we run out of places to explore together? Hardly. We have just rethought the unknown land that we seek. Today in the men's movement, many men see the place where no man has gone before as the place in which we have better relationships with our family and friends. This is a journey with its own perils and fears that many men choose to attempt. This new mythic ideal has its own notion of heroes and zanes that contemporary sociocultural forces helped usher into being. However, we are fooled if we believe that this will be the end of the journey of the evolving myth of masculinity. Sociocultural forces will again change, as they have for millennia, and this will lead to a yet another notion of ideal masculinity. Some changes will occur on a microlevel, affecting the fashion of the period for how men are suppose to conduct themselves. In this case, earlier versions of masculine paradigms may be reinvented (with a slightly new twist). And then, there may come a time when sociocultural forces press for a truly new paradigm of masculinity. Such periods in Western culture are the most impactive, and a new one will spur into existence truly new mythology to negotiate the experience.

THE EVOLVING MYTH OF MASCULINITY

Finally, I am a gender-role theorist, researcher, and psychologist who often argues for certain advances in gender-role freedom for men. I argue and sometimes cajole my students, patients, and myself that men will be better off if not constricted by the rigid roles that have come to dominate what men are supposed to be. What I have come to realize is that my approach represents the cultural paradigm in which I live. Just as in all cultural myths, people living within this paradigm struggle to see outside and to gain a perspective with objective eyes. That is, I have my own notions and biases about which paradigms have the most to offer. This book has been especially challenging as I try to move into and out of my own paradigm in my effort to gain perspective on what masculinity was and what it is becoming. I am most confident in the notion that our mythos has changed over time. Masculinity has changed its definition over time, and it will continue to do so.

Thomas Kuhn (1962) has mentioned that a scientific theory is often sustained for much longer than the theory warrants. I have made an argument that aspects of his use of the Hegelian dialectic model can be applied to the examination of a culture's gender roles. The major difference for which I argue is the blending of cultural paradigms of masculinity as opposed to completely replacing one with another. In this spirit, there will come a time when current cultural myths of masculinity will be outdated and perhaps forgotten, only to be remembered and then, perhaps, subsequently recycled. In this way, past cultural paradigms and their material are always available to be revisited, reworked, and reincorporated. One need only turn to the shelves of any modern bookstore to see how myths from more than 2,000 years ago find their way into contemporary paradigms.

This turning-back-to-Eden approach is unique to the cultural myths we create. In the physical sciences we believe the answers lie ahead of us, but in creating our cultural myth of masculinity and other social traditions we often focus our attention on the past, as a nostalgic time when life was ideal. Only when sociocultural forces so dictate do we move cautiously into the next truly new evolution of masculinity.

The examination of the cultural myth of masculinity points us to the ideals that we have held and currently hold as models for men. These are the vehicles for the time-honored purposes of descriptive and prescriptive education in regards to gender roles. They also reflect the struggles that will lead to the birth of the next evolution of masculinity.

REFERENCES

Abelin, E. (1971). The role of the father in the separation-individuation process. In J. B. McDevitt & C. F. Settlage (Eds.), *Separation individuation* (pp. 52–69). New York: International Universities Press.

Altman, D. (1972). *Homosexual: Oppression and liberation.* Sydney: Angus & Robertson.

Baring, A., & Cashford, J. (1993). *The myth of the goddess.* New York: Viking Penguin.

Bem, S. L. (1974). The measurement of psychological androgyny. *Journal of Consulting and Clinical Psychology, 42,* 155–162.

Betcher, R. W., & Pollack, W. S. (1993). *In a time of fallen heroes: The re-creation of masculinity.* New York: Atheneum.

Blazina, C. (1997). The fear of the feminine in the Western psyche and the masculine task of disidentification: Their effect on the development of masculine gender role conflict. *Journal of Men's Studies, 6,* 55–68.

Blazina, C. (2001). Analytic psychology and gender role conflict: The fragile masculine self. *Psychotherapy, 38,* 50–59.

Bleys, R. C. (1996). *The geography of perversion: Male-to-male sexual behaviour outside the West and the ethnographic imagination 1750–1918.* London: Cassell.

Bly, R. (1990). *Iron John.* Reading, MA: Addison-Wesley.

Campbell, J. K. (1956). *The hero with a thousand faces.* New York: Meridian.

Carnes, M. C., & Griffen, C. (Eds.). (1990). *Meaning of manhood: Constructions of masculinity in Victorian America.* Chicago: University of Chicago Press.

Chance, J. (1997). *Christine de Pizan's letter of Othea to Hector.* Rochester, New York: Boydell & Brewer.

Chauncey, G. (1982). "From sexual inversion to homosexuality: Medicine and the changing conceptualization of female deviancy." *Salmagundi, 58.*

Chodorow, N. (1978). *The reproduction of mothering: Psychoanalysis and the sociology of gender.* Berkeley: University of California Press.

Clatterbaugh, K. (1998). *Contemporary perspectives on masculinity: Men, women, and politics in modern society.* Boulder, CO: Westview Press.

Connell, R. W. (1995). *Masculinities.* Berkeley: University of California Press.

Davidson, H. R. E. (1965). *Gods and myths of northern Europe.* New York: Viking Penguin.

Dinerstein, D. (1976). *The mermaid and the minotaur: Sexual arrangements and human malaise.* New York: Harper & Row.

Dumézil, G. (1970). *The destiny of the warrior.* Chicago: University of Chicago Press.

Dumézil, G. (1973). *Gods of the ancient Northmen.* Berkeley: University of California Press.

Eisler, R. (1988). *The chalice and the blade: Our history, our future.* New York: HarperCollins.

Ellis, H. (1936). *Studies in the psychology of sex, vol. 1–7.* New York: Random House.

Ellis, H., & Symonds, J. A. (1897). *Sexual inversion.* London: Wilson and Macmillan. Reprint, New York: Arno Press, 1975.

Erisman, F. (1997). The enduring myth and the modern west. In G. D. Nash & R. W. Etulain (Eds.), *Researching Western history: Topics in the twentieth century.* Albuquerque: University of New Mexico Press.

Farrell, W. (1987). *The myth of male power: Why men are the disposable sex.* New York: Simon and Schuster.

Fitzgerald. F. S. (1925). *The great Gatsby.* New York: Simon and Schuster Trade.

Foucault, M. (1980). *History of sexuality.* New York: Vintage.

Franklin, C. W., II (1994a). Ain't I a man?: The efficacy of black masculinities for men's studies in the 1990's. In R. G. Majors & J. V. Gordon (Eds.), *The American black male and his present status and his future* (pp. 271–283). Chicago: Nelson Hall.

Franklin, C. W., II (1994b). Men's studies, the men's movement, and the study of black masculinities: Further demystifying of masculinities in America. In R. G. Majors & J. V. Gordon (Eds.), *The American black male and his present status and his future* (pp. 3–19). Chicago: Nelson Hall.

Frantz, J. B., & Choate, J. E. (1955). *The American cowboy.* Norman: University of Oklahoma Press.

Frazer, J. G. (1922). *The golden bough.* London: Macmillan.

Freud, S. (1963). Observations on wild analysis. In P. Rieff (Ed.), *Freud: Therapy and technique.* New York: Collier Books. (Original work published 1910).

Gathorne-Hardy, J. (1978). *The old school tie.* New York: Viking Press.

Gimbutas, M. (1989). *Language of the goddess: Unearthing the hidden symbols of Western civilization.* San Francisco: HarperSanFrancisco.

Gimbutas, M. (1991). *The civilization of the goddess.* San Francisco: HarperSanFrancisco.

Girouard, M. (1981). *The return to Camelot: Chivalry and the English gentleman.* New Haven, CT: Yale University Press.

Greenson, R. (1968). Disidentifying from mother: Its special importance for the boy. *International Journal of Psychoanalysis, 49,* 370–374.

Guts Muth, J. C. F. (1880). *Gymnastics for youth; Or, a practical guide to healthful and amusing exercises for the use of schools* (C. G. Salzmann, Trans.). London: J. Johnson. (Original work published 1804).

Hanning, R. W. (1972). The social significance of the 12th century chivalric romance. *Mediaevalia et Humanistica, 3,* 3–29.

Haudry, J. H. (1999). *The Indo-Europeans.* Washington, DC: Scott-Townsend.

Hawkes, J. (1958). *Dawn of the Gods.* London: Chatto and Windus.

Heaney, S. (2000). *Beowulf: A new translation.* New York: Farrar, Straus, and Giroux.

Hering, G. F. (Ed.). (1931). Goethe an Herder. *Genius der Jugend.* Stuttgart and Hamburg.

Highwater, J. (1991). *Myth and sexuality.* New York: Meridian.

Horner, A. J. (1984). *Treating the Oedipal patient in brief psychotherapy.* New York: Jason Aronson.

Horney, K. (1932). The dread of women. *International Journal of Psychoanalysis, 13,* 348–360.

Horrocks, R. (1994). *Masculinity in crisis: Myths, fantasies, and realities.* New York: St. Martin's Press.

Jaeger, C. S. (1985). *The origins of courtliness: Civilizing trends and the formation of courtly ideals, 939–1210.* Philadelphia: University of Pennsylvania Press.

Jahn, F. L. (1816). German gymnastics. In G. L. Mosse (Ed.), *The image of man: The creation of modern masculinity.* New York: Oxford University Press.

Johnson, R. A. (1974). *He: Understanding masculine psychology.* New York: Harper & Row.

Jung, C. G. (1953). Animus and anima. *Collected works* (Vol. 7). New York: Pantheon Books.

Jung, C. G. (1954). Concerning the archetypes with special reference to the anima concept. *Collected works* (Vol. 9). New York: Pantheon Books.

Jung, C. G. (1956). Symbols of transformation. *Collected works* (Vol. 5). New York: Pantheon Books.

Keen, M. (1984). *Chivalry.* New Haven, CT: Yale University Press.

Keiser, E. B. (1997). *Courtly desire and medial homophobia.* New Haven, CT: Yale University Press.

Kingsley, C. (1856). *The heroes; Or, Greek fairy tales.* Cambridge, England: Macmillan.

Krafft-Ebing, R. von. (1886/1903). *Psychopathia sexualis with especial reference to antipathic sexual instinct: A medico-forensic study.* Philadelphia: F.A. Davis.

Krull, M. (1986). *Freud and his father.* New York: Norton.

Kuhn, T. S. (1962). *The structure of scientific revolutions.* Chicago: University of Chicago Press.

Kupfersmid, J. (1993). Freud's rationale for abandoning the seduction theory. *Psychoanalytic Psychology, 10,* 275–290.

Kupfersmid, J. (1995). Does the Oedipus complex exist? *Psychotherapy, 32,* 535–547.

Levant, R. F. (1992). Toward the reconstruction of masculinity. *Journal of Family Psychology, 5,* 379–402.

Levinson, D. J., Darrow, C. N., Klein, E. B., Levinson, M. H., & McKee, B. (1978). *The seasons of a man's life.* New York: Knopf.

Lincoln, B. (1991). *Death, war, and sacrifice: Studies in ideology and practice.* Chicago: University of Chicago Press.

Linton, R. (1957). *Tree of culture.* New York: Knopf.

Littleton, C. S. (1982). *The new comparative mythology.* Berkeley: University of California Press.

Mahler, M. S., & Gosliner, R. J. (1955). On symbiotic child psychosis: Genetic, dynamic, and restitutive aspects. *Psychoanalytic Study of the Child, 10,* 195–212.

Mallory, J. P. (1991). *In search of the Indo-Europeans: Language, archaeology, and myth.* London: Thames and Hudson.

Mallory, T. (1972). *The death of King Arthur (La Mort le roi Artu)* (James Cable, Trans.). New York: Penguin.

Mason, J. (1984). *The assault on the truth.* New York: Penguin.

McCreary, D. (1994). The male role and avoiding femininity. *Sex Roles, 31,* 517–531.

McMurtry, L. (1986). *Lonesome dove.* New York: Simon and Schuster Trade.

Meade, M. (1993). *Men and the water of life.* San Francisco: HarperSanFrancisco.

Meerloo, J. A. M. (1968). The psychological role of the father: The father cuts the cord. *Child and Family,* 102–116.

Monmouth, G. of (1997). *The history of the kings of Britain* (Lewis Thorpe, Trans.). New York: Viking Penguin.

Moore, R., & Gillette, D. (1991). *King, warrior, magician, lover: Rediscovering the archetypes of the mature masculine.* San Francisco: HarperSanFrancisco.

Mosse, G. L. (1996). *The image of man: The creation of modern masculinity.* New York: Oxford University Press.

O'Neil, J. M. (1982). Gender role conflict and strain in men's lives: Implications for psychiatrists, psychologists, and other human service providers. In K. Solomon & N. B. Levy (Eds.), *Men in transition* (pp. 5–40). New York: Plenum Press.

O'Neil, J. M., Helms, B. J., Gable, R. K., David, L., & Wrightsman, L. S. (1986). Gender role conflict scale: College men's fear of femininity. *Sex Roles, 14,* 335–350.

Osherson, S. (1986). *Finding our fathers.* New York: Fawcett Columbine.

Palmer, L. R. (1956). The concept of social obligation in Indo-European: A study in structural semantics. *Hommages à Max Niederman,* coll. Latomus, 23: 258–269.

Pearson, R. (1973). Some aspects of social mobility in early historic Indo-European societies. *Journal of Indo-European Studies, 1,* 155–162.

Pendergast, T. (2000). *Creating the modern man: American magazines and consumer culture.* Columbia: University of Missouri Press.

Pleck, J. H. (1981). *The myth of masculinity.* Cambridge, MA: MIT Press.

Pleck, J. H., Sonenstein, F. L., & Ku, L. C. (1993). Masculinity ideology and its correlates. In S. Oskamp & M. Costanzo (Eds.), *Gender issues in contemporary society* (pp. 85–110). Newbury Park, CA: Sage.

Pollack, W. S. (1995). No man is an island: Toward a new psychoanalytic psychology of men. In R. F. Levant & W. S. Pollack (Eds.), *A new psychology of men* (pp. 33–67). New York: Basic Books.

Pollack, W. S. (1998). *Real boys: Rescuing our sons from the myths of boyhood.* New York: Henry Holt.

Prosser, J. (1998). Transsexuals and transsexologists: Inversion and the emergence of transsexual subjectivity. In L. Bland & L. Doran (Eds.), *Sexology in culture.* Cambridge, England: Polity Press.

Puhvel, J. (1987). *Comparative mythology.* Maryland: Johns Hopkins University Press.

Raglan, L. (1956). *The hero: A study in tradition, myth, and drama.* New York: Vintage.

Rank, O. (1914/1959). *The myth of the birth of hero.* New York: Vintage.

Rowan, J. (1987). *Horned god: Feminism and men as wounding and healing.* New York: Routledge.

Ruck, C. A. P., & Staples, D. (1994). *World of classical myth: Gods and goddesses, heroines and heroes.* Durham, NC: North Carolina Academic Press.

Segal, R. A. (1990). *In quest of the hero.* Princeton, NJ: Princeton University Press.

Sergent, B. (1984). *Homosexuality in Greek myth.* Boston: Beacon Press.

Shakespeare, W. (1988). *Henry V.* New York: Bantam Doubleday Dell.

Sjoestedt, M. (1982). *Gods and heroes of the Celts.* Berkeley, CA: Turtle Island Foundation.

Slotkin, R. (1985). *The fatal environment: The myth of the frontier in the age of industrialization, 1800–1890.* Norman: University of Oklahoma Press.

Solt, G. C. (1996). A view from inside: Ronald Fairbairn's contribution to men's self-understanding. *Journal of Men's Studies, 5,* 31–47.

Spretnak, C. (1978). *Lost goddesses of early Greece: A collection of pre-Hellenic myths.* Boston: Beacon Press.

Storr, M. (1998). Transformations: Subjects, categories, and cures in Krafft-Ebings's sexology. In L. Bland & L. Doran (Eds.), *Sexology in culture.* Cambridge, England: Polity Press.

Tacitus, C. (1999). *Germania* (J. B. Rives, Trans.). New York: Oxford University Press.

Terman, L., & Miles, C. (1936). *Sex and personality.* New York: McGraw-Hill.

Webb, W. P. (1931). *The great plains.* New York: Grosset & Dunlap.

Weston, J. (1985). *The real American cowboy.* New York: New Amsterdam Books.

Weston, J. L. (1993). *From ritual to romance.* Princeton, NJ: Princeton University Press. (Original work published 1920).

White, K. (1993). *The first sexual revolution: The emergence of male heterosexuality in modern America.* New York: New York University Press.

Winn, S. M. M. (1995). *Heaven, heroes, and happiness: The Indo-European roots of Western ideology.* Washington, DC: University Press of America.

Wister, O. (1895). The evolution of the cowpuncher. *Harper's Monthly,* Sept., 608.

Wister, O. (1968). *The Virginian: A horseman of the plains.* New York: Dodd, Mead. (Original work published 1902).

Wolohojian, A. M. (1969). *Romance of Alexander.* New York: Columbia University Press.

INDEX

About the Author

CHRIS BLAZINA is an Assistant Professor of Educational Psychology
at The University of Houston.